The Good Morning Text

• • •

A 365-Day Journey to Get Closer to Who You Really Are

DANNI HEARTS

I take the time to dedicate this book to three amazing people in my life; two that are living and one that has passed on. The dynamic of love these three people have showed me in my lifetime has allowed my heart to soar on a path to self-love and finding who I truly am in this big world.

Nathan- I want you to know that whatever you choose in life, I love you and always will. You have brought so much joy to my life and I am grateful to call you my brother.

Makara- Thank you for teaching me so much about my purpose in life and beginning the amazing journey I am on today.

Charlie- Your love could never be replaced. You began my spiritual journey three weeks before you passed on, and for that I am forever grateful. You are the definition of unconditional love.

Thank you all for taking this beautiful journey with me as we become closer to ourselves. This is the definition of self-love!

Foreword:

Good morning. How did you sleep last night? Did you sleep through the night, or did the terror and fears of the world we live in turn you into an insomniac? No matter where you fall on that spectrum, we should all be able to agree on one thing; a new morning brings the hope of a new beginning, and maybe even a new life.

Each day the sun rises, we rise with it. The conflicts that the world brings us on a daily basis can weigh on us like cement in a swimming pool, and when that happens, it's easy to sink into our beds and drown within the morning. Have you ever felt like that? That feeling that you can't get out of bed because you'd rather not swim through the deep waters of what the world has in store for you once you place your two feet on its surface.

The morning is the catalyst to our story as humans. Each day a new story is written in our lives and as our eyes open, chapter one begins and the next adventure awaits. So if you're chapter begins with "forget this stuff" what does that mean for the rest of your day... your life? They say breakfast is the most important meal of the day. If your breakfast is filling and nutritious, the assumption is that your body is now fully prepared to take on the day. If you wake up and eat the leftover chicken breast, that you didn't microwave, the day might not go as smooth as you envisioned, I can guarantee you that.

So, if your body needs the right food to function properly, your brain needs just as much attention to get the day started. What do you decide to watch in the morning? How hot or cold is the water you wash with? Do you listen to music to get motivated, or do you pray?

All valid questions, but let's back up... how do you start your morning when you first open your eyes... the moment when you realize you have been given another day to live.

It was in 2015 when I found myself in this very situation. I would lay in my twin bed, eyes wide open, searching for a reason to get out of bed. I was 26, living in Southern California, working on a film degree. Ok, I know what you're thinking... my situation sounds ideal, and I should have more than few reasons to get out of bed. I agree, but my morning issues weren't based on lack of purpose, I suffered from a far more potent poison... loneliness.

I moved to California on what seemed like a whim and with all my friends and family on the east coast, my constant state of isolation ate up anytime that wasn't spent on school. To make matters worse, most of it the alone time was self-imposed because of a constant paranoia of people in a different area; a reflex of growing up in the inner city. Over time, I developed an instinct to distrust people and question their motives which led to crippling fear, a fear that kept me in my bed every morning, eyes opened, mentally drained.

Then one morning, everything changed. I got a text message from one of my best friends in the world. The opening simply read "Good Morning" and the words that followed contained a heartfelt and inspiring message. I can't recall the exact words, I only remember the feeling. That feeling was hope... connection... encouragement. For the first time in a long time, I felt like getting out of bed. Now I ended up going back to sleep, but that was only because California is three hours behind Philadelphia, and my friends were slow to adjust to my new sleeping patterns.

I thought the message was random, but I thanked my friend and appreciated the feeling that her message gave me. Then the next morning I got a text, then the next morning same thing, and after a while, every morning that followed, I woke up to a good morning text, filled with inspiration and connection. Now by this point, I figured that I wasn't the only one to receive these messages to start my morning, but that was ok. Whoever my friend decided would make this list of morning texts, I knew we were all lucky to have someone who took a little time out of her morning to share good vibes. It's those small ripples in the ocean that can eventually create a wave. My wave led to my entire mood changing in California. I got more social, I took my chances, and I embraced my time in the exodus. Sure there were other factors that led to me opening up, but the seed was that one text, that one morning.

That friend of mine is also the author of this book. I suggested that these morning messages weren't meant to live and die on our cell phone screens, but instead, they need to be shared with the world, so the next person can find a reason to get out of bed in the morning. I guarantee you that after you read this book, you will feel like Danni is one of your best friends too.

Robert Bell III

Everyone is looking for that Good Morning Text. That text that lights up your world ensuring a beautiful day ahead. That text people look forward to in the morning validating feelings of belonging and love. Search for it no longer. No more worrying if that other person is thinking of you. No more faking, hiding, or dimming your light at the expense of others. It is all about you. Live in your trueness and let go of any judgement you have towards yourself and others. It is time to reach new depths of who you truly are … Let these next 365 days take you there… ARE YOU READY?

At this time, I would like you to write down where you are in life currently and where you would like to see yourself a year from now. As you complete the book, you will be asked the same question to see where this 365-day journey has taken you. Be open-minded and real with yourself. It is the only way this will work, so take that mask off and be who you always were intended to be. Just be the real you!

_____

_____

_____

_____

_____

_____

LET THE JOURNEY BEGIN ☺

Good Morning...

Know deep in your heart that you are one amazing person with qualities one could only wish for. It is time to let them shine. Do not let anything hold you back from your greatness.

What is dimming your light from experiencing full greatness?

_____

_____

_____

_____

_____

_____

_____

_____

_____

_____

_____

Good Morning...

Have faith that endless opportunities for prosperity and happiness are right ahead. Do not feed into the lies. You deserve the best of anything this life has to offer. Never forget that.

What does prosperity look like for you?

_____

_____

_____

_____

_____

_____

_____

_____

_____

_____

_____

Good Morning...

You must know in your heart that someone in this world can see your beauty, even if your exterior is a beast with feelings of hurt; unable to express, instead only lashing out when too much exist. Understand that under that exterior you are displayed as one beautiful person.

What has caused you to develop the exterior you present to others? Is it different than the person you are when you are truly with yourself?

_____

_____

_____

_____

_____

_____

_____

_____

_____

_____

_____

Good Morning...

Love is not something that should only be given on one single day. Love should be given every day without any hesitations. Make sure to say "I love you" to the ones closest to your heart, for life is so much easier with love.

What is your true definition of love?

_____

_____

_____

_____

_____

_____

_____

_____

_____

_____

_____

_____

Good Morning...

Take risks knowing tomorrow is not promised, for life is more adventurous when you live outside the box.

What risks are you willing to take to live a more adventurous life?

_____

_____

_____

_____

_____

_____

_____

_____

_____

_____

_____

_____

_____

Good Morning...

Why wait for tomorrow what you can accomplish today, for people who put things off for another day never reach their full potential. You deserve to be your best self every day.

What have you been putting off that you should be working on accomplishing?

_____

_____

_____

_____

_____

_____

_____

_____

_____

_____

_____

_____

Good Morning...

Bring in each new day with positive vibes and wonderful energy. Negativity will always try to find a way to control you, but you are stronger than any obstacle that lies ahead. Always remember that!

What affects your vibes and energy? What makes you feel unlike yourself?

_____

_____

_____

_____

_____

_____

_____

_____

_____

_____

_____

Good Morning...

Your happiness is a choice only you can make daily. It is solely a responsibility of your own. Embrace all the ways to make yourself happy because that is what matters most in the world.

What truly makes you happy?

_____

_____

_____

_____

_____

_____

_____

_____

_____

_____

_____

Good Morning...

Do not let your traumatized past lead you to believe you are not worthy of an amazing future. Embrace the hardships allowing you to appreciate life in a whole new way.

What hardships are you currently experiencing? What steps are you taking to overcome them?

_____

_____

_____

_____

_____

_____

_____

_____

_____

_____

_____

Good Morning...

True happiness and positive vibes keep the world going round. If you are unhappy and surrounded by negativity, change it, for life is more meaningful when you allow yourself to be freed.

What does freedom look like to you?

_____

_____

_____

_____

_____

_____

_____

_____

_____

_____

_____

_____

Good Morning…

Never rely on others to show you love and happiness. Go after it yourself. Allowing someone that type of power over you may result in a feeling of emptiness over time. Fill yourself with love and you will never lack anything.

What do you love about being the amazing person you are?

_____

_____

_____

_____

_____

_____

_____

_____

_____

_____

_____

_____

Good Morning...

Let yourself be freed from the bondage that has been holding you back, for you do not deserve to be held down anymore.

What would you consider the bondage in your life? How are you setting yourself free?

_____

_____

_____

_____

_____

_____

_____

_____

_____

_____

_____

_____

_____

Good Morning…

This is your world. You hold the key to your life. You are the ruler of your destiny. No longer be held down by the misery in this world. Rise above it knowing with love we can do all things.

Describe your world if you were genuinely happy. No trauma. No past. No body shaming. No heartache. Just pure happiness. Use all your senses to describe this world. Challenge is to begin to create these ideas into your physical world.

_____

_____

_____

_____

_____

_____

_____

_____

_____

_____

Good Morning…

Love with all your heart. Not fearing the unknown is what sets you apart from the rest.

What causes you to fear things in life?

_____

_____

_____

_____

_____

_____

_____

_____

_____

_____

_____

_____

Good Morning...

Trust the journey you are currently on and never give up, for life has a beautiful way of surprising you once you begin believing in yourself.

What part of your journey are you currently on?

_____

_____

_____

_____

_____

_____

_____

_____

_____

_____

_____

_____

_____

Good Morning…

Do not get upset when people are not truthful with you. Smile because you can walk away with your head high knowing you deserve better.

What do you believe you deserve in life?

_____

_____

_____

_____

_____

_____

_____

_____

_____

_____

_____

_____

Good Morning...

Continue speaking positivity into the universe and watch how your life changes in dynamic ways, for negativity and doubt only hinder blessings.

Use this space to speak some life into yourself today. Inspire yourself to do amazing things.

_____

_____

_____

_____

_____

_____

_____

_____

_____

_____

_____

_____

Good Morning...

Tomorrow, life, as you know it, can be changed drastically without any warning. Make sure to smile and love more. Having the ability to do these two things allows your soul to come alive. Be free in love.

What makes you smile?

_____

_____

_____

_____

_____

_____

_____

_____

_____

_____

_____

_____

_____

Good Morning...

Do not be a slave to negativity, for it has a way of hindering your blessings.

What negativity do you have to let go of to reach your ultimate blessings?

_____

_____

_____

_____

_____

_____

_____

_____

_____

_____

_____

Good Morning...

As time prolongs, one may come to realize that what is truly needed to survive in this cruel world is... LOVE!!! Love more knowing that is what you were born to do without ever feeling bad for doing so.

How is love represented in your own life?

_____

_____

_____

_____

_____

_____

_____

_____

_____

_____

_____

Good Morning...

When you love yourself properly, you begin to shine differently. Love yourself for the amazing person you are. Everything is unfolding beautifully. Just have faith.

What do you sincerely love about yourself and why?

_____

_____

_____

_____

_____

_____

_____

_____

_____

_____

Good Morning…

Never question why something is happening in your life, for each thing thrown your way comes with a major lesson.

What major lesson are you learning as of today?

_____

_____

_____

_____

_____

_____

_____

_____

_____

_____

_____

Good Morning...

Set yourself free and heal yourself with the most important love there is in this world: YOUR OWN. It is time to give yourself what you need without guilt or shame. It is time for more self-love.

What are you currently healing from or still need healing from?

_____

_____

_____

_____

_____

_____

_____

_____

_____

_____

_____

Good Morning...

Many people do not have half of what you have, but continue to live with peace in their minds and love in their hearts. It should be a daily reminder to never take time or this life for granted anymore.

What provides you with peace of mind and love in your heart?

_____

_____

_____

_____

_____

_____

_____

_____

_____

_____

_____

_____

Good Morning...

There are so many things one could be thankful for on this beautiful day. Hope this day brings nothing but happiness and laughter because who deserves it more than you? No one!

What makes you thankful on a regular basis?

_____

_____

_____

_____

_____

_____

_____

_____

_____

_____

_____

Good Morning...

If no one told you today, let me be the first to say that you are amazingly created for greatness. Anything or anyone that does not make you feel this way does not deserve to be within your space.

What makes you amazing and separate from the rest?

_____

_____

_____

_____

_____

_____

_____

_____

_____

_____

_____

_____

Good Morning...

Honor the beauty that surrounds you daily. Celebrate the very things that provide you with life. Be thankful for everything you have been given.

Name all the things worth celebrating life for.

_____

_____

_____

_____

_____

_____

_____

_____

_____

_____

_____

_____

Good Morning...

The journey you are on, called life, is meant to build character, increase personal growth, and provide the drive to keep pushing. Do not lose your motivation to keep moving forward, for you are your best asset.

What is your motivation to keep moving forward?

_____

_____

_____

_____

_____

_____

_____

_____

_____

_____

_____

_____

_____

Good Morning...

Setbacks only prove to us that something bigger is ahead. Stay clear from filling your mind with worry or doubt. It does not add any growth to your value.

How much do you value yourself?

_____

_____

_____

_____

_____

_____

_____

_____

_____

_____

_____

_____

Good Morning...

Live in the present and not the past. Moments get lost when we focus on what previously happened instead of what the universe has in store for us.

What present are you currently living?

_____

_____

_____

_____

_____

_____

_____

_____

_____

_____

_____

_____

_____

Good Morning...

Do not be sad that something has ended. Smile knowing you get the opportunity to start a new chapter. Be grateful for the moments you are given and take the lesson learned with you.

What new chapter are you declaring to start today to become a better you? Get creative with this chapter and make sure to explore this question without judgement towards yourself. Be free in becoming the best you.

_____

_____

_____

_____

_____

_____

_____

_____

_____

_____

Good Morning…

Pay attention to the little miracles that are happening around you, for coincidences are blessings in disguise.

What makes you second-guess yourself at times?

_____

_____

_____

_____

_____

_____

_____

_____

_____

_____

_____

_____

_____

Good Morning...

Life does not stop for anyone, so make sure to keep moving. Embrace the changes and remind yourself that a bigger plan is already in motion. You got this. Just believe!

What makes it so hard to deal with any type of change in your life?

_____

_____

_____

_____

_____

_____

_____

_____

_____

_____

_____

Good Morning...

Never give up on your dreams. It may take longer than expected or obstacles may arise, but your dream is important, nonetheless. There are many paths that lead to the same big road. Find another route knowing your dreams are the ultimate destination.

How many routes are you willing to take to reach your goals and why?

_____

_____

_____

_____

_____

_____

_____

_____

_____

_____

_____

_____

_____

Good Morning…

May you have one amazing day knowing you can accomplish anything with a positive mindset.

What is your current state of mind? Does it reflect how you genuinely want to live in life?

_____

_____

_____

_____

_____

_____

_____

_____

_____

_____

Good Morning...

Let your mind, body, and soul be freed daily. Being a prisoner within yourself keeps you captured in the realms of society.

What allows you to lessen the burden on your soul?

_____

_____

_____

_____

_____

_____

_____

_____

_____

_____

_____

_____

Good Morning...

There were no mistakes created when you were brought into this world. Every imperfection and flaw were perfectly placed to make a beautiful person like you. You are a blessing. Embrace it. Know it and never question it.

Take a moment to explain all the beautiful parts of yourself.

_____

_____

_____

_____

_____

_____

_____

_____

_____

_____

_____

Good Morning...

There is no better time than the present to manifest your dreams. Align yourself with the way you think, feel, and believe to bring forth your deepest desires. Do not let the obstacles distract you.

What changes do you need to make, starting today, to align yourself with your dreams and desires?

_____

_____

_____

_____

_____

_____

_____

_____

_____

_____

_____

_____

Good Morning…

Be sure to start each day by speaking positivity into the universe and into your own life. You receive what you put into the world.

What can you do to change your energy when you are feeling low?

_____

_____

_____

_____

_____

_____

_____

_____

_____

_____

_____

Good Morning...

When the obstacles arrive in your life, do not hold back in fear. Rise up in love knowing that you are meant to do great things in this world. These are all lessons along the way. Appreciate them to see better days.

If you knew you could not fail, what great thing would you accomplish right now and why?

_____

_____

_____

_____

_____

_____

_____

_____

_____

_____

Good Morning…

When you give yourself the opportunity to love without any fears, that's when life truly begins.

What parts of yourself do you need to love more?

_____

_____

_____

_____

_____

_____

_____

_____

_____

_____

_____

_____

Good Morning...

Life may seem chaotic right now, but you will realize in time all you've ever been through brought you to this point.

What holds you back from fully believing in yourself at times?

_____

_____

_____

_____

_____

_____

_____

_____

_____

_____

_____

_____

Good Morning...

Do not let yourself to be changed by this world. Be proud of who you are, regardless of the circumstance.

What makes you proud to be yourself?

_____

_____

_____

_____

_____

_____

_____

_____

_____

_____

_____

_____

Good Morning...

There were no mistakes made when you were born. You are perfectly imperfect wrapped up in such a beautiful essence. Accept yourself for who you truly are. Only then will you see your true beauty.

Who are you? How do you define yourself?

_____

_____

_____

_____

_____

_____

_____

_____

_____

_____

_____

_____

Good Morning...

Do what you love daily without any feelings of obligation, for with passion comes freedom.

What do you passionately love to do in this life?

_____

_____

_____

_____

_____

_____

_____

_____

_____

_____

_____

_____

_____

Good Morning…

If something makes you sincerely happy, never question it. The true definition of living comes with countless reasons to enjoy life.

How do you enjoy life being within your own company?

_____

_____

_____

_____

_____

_____

_____

_____

_____

_____

_____

_____

_____

Good Morning...

Giving up should never be an option when you want something bad enough. Be optimistic knowing in your heart that things will get better.

Are you worth giving up on yourself? Why or why not?

_____

_____

_____

_____

_____

_____

_____

_____

_____

_____

_____

_____

_____

Good Morning…

Follow your heart, regardless of what happens in life, for it will never stir you wrong.

Why is it hard at times for you to listen to your heart rather than your mind?

_____

_____

_____

_____

_____

_____

_____

_____

_____

_____

_____

_____

Good Morning…

Take advantage of all the wonders life has to offer you without limitations. Limitations are driven by fear when we are all made of love.

What limits have you placed onto your own life?

_____

_____

_____

_____

_____

_____

_____

_____

_____

_____

_____

_____

_____

Good Morning...

When there's love in one's heart, the concept of life changes. Allow yourself to love and be loved in return, for there is no better feeling in this world.

What prevents you from loving wholeheartedly?

_____

_____

_____

_____

_____

_____

_____

_____

_____

_____

_____

_____

Good Morning...

You are provided daily with life because your purpose here on Earth has not been fulfilled yet. You are more than what society teaches and you have the capability to achieve anything that your heart desires. Always believe this.

What do you believe is your purpose here on this Earth?

_____

_____

_____

_____

_____

_____

_____

_____

_____

_____

_____

_____

Good Morning...

Take a moment to realize who you are. For you are... strong, wise, bold, determined, and so much more. You have overcome some big obstacles and guess what? You are still standing. Give yourself more credit and stop being so hard on yourself. You are doing magnificent at this thing we call "life."

What causes you to doubt yourself at times in life?

_____

_____

_____

_____

_____

_____

_____

_____

_____

_____

_____

_____

Good Morning...

Understand that at times things may not happen when you want them to, but that does not mean they will never happen. Have faith in the outcome while continuing the journey. The process is how you get there.

Where does your faith lie?

_____

_____

_____

_____

_____

_____

_____

_____

_____

_____

_____

Good Morning...

The ups and downs in your life just add to your amazing testimony that one day may save someone's life. Take pride in who you are.

What is your story?

_____

_____

_____

_____

_____

_____

_____

_____

_____

_____

_____

_____

_____

_____

Good Morning...

Never lose sight of what drives or motivates you because when passion exists anything is possible.

Name all the things or people who drive or motivate you.

_____

_____

_____

_____

_____

_____

_____

_____

_____

_____

_____

_____

_____

Good Morning...

Life, as you know it, continues to evolve. Embrace all the goodness while shielding yourself from all the chaos. You were not created to be destroyed.

What chaos is holding you back from evolving?

_____

_____

_____

_____

_____

_____

_____

_____

_____

_____

_____

_____

Good Morning…

Do not continue to waste your precious energy on the things the universe can take care of. Focus on love and happiness, and the universe will always see you through.

What has been your focus recently? Has it been helping or hindering your growth?

_____

_____

_____

_____

_____

_____

_____

_____

_____

_____

_____

_____

Good Morning...

As you open your eyes today, be blessed. Materialistic things can break or fade, but love lives forever.

Who or what should you be showing more love to and why?

_____

_____

_____

_____

_____

_____

_____

_____

_____

_____

_____

_____

_____

Good Morning...

This world will continue to rob you of the joy you deserve, if you allow it. It is time for change. It is time to wake up daily knowing failures do occur, but they only make you stronger.

Name a failure you learned a mighty lesson from and how it made you stronger.

_____

_____

_____

_____

_____

_____

_____

_____

_____

_____

_____

_____

Good Morning...

Take chances knowing without trying true happiness cannot be gained. Give yourself a fresh start today.

What does taking a chance look like for you?

_____

_____

_____

_____

_____

_____

_____

_____

_____

_____

_____

_____

_____

Good Morning...

Stop comparing your life to the next person's, for each person's story has a different ending. Be grateful for the life you have been provided with flaws and all.

Use this space to write 10 "I AM" statements reminding you of who you are.

_____

_____

_____

_____

_____

_____

_____

_____

_____

_____

_____

_____

Good Morning...

Trust that all things in life will be worked out with patience and gratitude. Never lose sight of your dreams. When you least expect it, fulfillment arrives.

Where do you see yourself in five years?

_____

_____

_____

_____

_____

_____

_____

_____

_____

_____

_____

_____

Good Morning...

When life tries to bring you down, find all the reasons to stand tall, for life has a way of blessing us after timeless amounts of efforts are made.

What would you sacrifice to receive the blessing you always wanted?

_____

_____

_____

_____

_____

_____

_____

_____

_____

_____

_____

_____

_____

Good morning...

Take time today to look in the mirror and admire the wonderful person that stares back at you. If you do not see that wonderful person, how do you expect someone else to? Love yourself starting today.

Name all positive attributes about yourself.

_____

_____

_____

_____

_____

_____

_____

_____

_____

_____

_____

Good Morning...

While others are rejoicing in your frustration, just smile because no one deserves you getting out of character. You are always in control. Keep that in mind.

What causes you to feel out of control?

_____

_____

_____

_____

_____

_____

_____

_____

_____

_____

_____

_____

Good Morning...

All the sweat, blood, and tears throughout this journey were all a part of a bigger plan. You've come too far ahead to let your dreams slip away now. Keep pushing on. A person is only as strong as their beliefs are.

What mindset do you currently have?

_____

_____

_____

_____

_____

_____

_____

_____

_____

_____

_____

Good Morning...

When you find something good, learn to flow with patience. There is something so precious in the fight that keeps the flame burning forever.

What flame are you currently burning in your life? Is it one of positivity or negativity?

_____

_____

_____

_____

_____

_____

_____

_____

_____

_____

_____

_____

Good Morning...

Love is what keeps this world going, so put the negativity aside. Without love, there will only be misery and you deserve more than that.

What misery are you currently trying to get out of?

_____

_____

_____

_____

_____

_____

_____

_____

_____

_____

_____

_____

_____

Good Morning...

It is time we stepped out of our comfort zones to accomplish what is said to be impossible. Believe in yourself that you can never fail, for learning only occurs when you take a chance.

What are you comfort zones and what are you willing to do to get out of them?

_____

_____

_____

_____

_____

_____

_____

_____

_____

_____

_____

Good Morning...

Life is too short to allow yourself to miss the opportunity to live. Society has created a way to keep people never satisfied, wanting more and more. Embrace more love because that is all we need.

Name all the things you love in life. Even the things you no longer do, but did as a kid. Those things are still a part of you. Awaken your inner child today!

_____

_____

_____

_____

_____

_____

_____

_____

_____

_____

_____

Good Morning...

Take matters into your own hands and be better than you were yesterday. The only person you should be in competition with is you, so never restrict yourself from your own greatness.

What restrictions have you placed on yourself that does not allow you to reach your full potential?

_____

_____

_____

_____

_____

_____

_____

_____

_____

_____

_____

Good Morning…

Always remember anything worth having requires sacrifices to reach a new level of happiness.

What is your current level of happiness?

_____

_____

_____

_____

_____

_____

_____

_____

_____

_____

_____

_____

Good Morning...

Admit when you are wrong and do not let pride stand in your way, for forgiveness displays growth in oneself.

Who or what do you need to forgive to grow more in life?

_____

_____

_____

_____

_____

_____

_____

_____

_____

_____

_____

_____

Good Morning...

Give yourself the ability to feel. Becoming numb does not allow you to experience all the positive and beautiful things this life has to offer.

What is something you do not like to think about due to the way it makes you feel? Create a plan to work through these emotions to no longer allow it to have power over you.

_____

_____

_____

_____

_____

_____

_____

_____

_____

_____

_____

_____

Good Morning...

Stop waiting for another moment to pass you by before you take another step. We must start believing in ourselves and not let others tell us what we can or cannot do. The time is now to take that leap of faith. Are you ready?

What makes it hard to believe in yourself at times?

_____

_____

_____

_____

_____

_____

_____

_____

_____

_____

_____

Good Morning…

When life takes a left turn unexpectedly, understand it will hurt, but you were created with strength. Keep living life to the fullest, even when it gets tough, for that shows true determination.

How would you define your strength?

_____

_____

_____

_____

_____

_____

_____

_____

_____

_____

_____

_____

Good Morning...

You are a perfect example of a king/queen. This world will tell you something different, but you are royalty. Live in your truth and always know who you truly are.

What is your truth?

_____

_____

_____

_____

_____

_____

_____

_____

_____

_____

_____

Good Morning...

We cannot stop what the heart is feeling. All we can do is live through these moments. Trust your heart always knowing it is all out of love. The heart never lies. Never forget that!

What makes your heart overwhelmed with love?

_____

_____

_____

_____

_____

_____

_____

_____

_____

_____

Good Morning...

Before you start to comment on someone else's problems, have yours taken care of. Why would someone take advice from someone who continues to make the same mistakes? Only a fool.

What mistakes do you continue to live through?

_____

_____

_____

_____

_____

_____

_____

_____

_____

_____

_____

_____

Good Morning...

You have an abundant amount of potential inside of you. Search deep within to find it. Once you do, just know you truly become limitless.

What do you consider to be your limits?

_____

_____

_____

_____

_____

_____

_____

_____

_____

_____

_____

_____

Good Morning...

Speak life into the world and it will come back to you ten times greater. Speak negativity into the world and watch yourself crumble.

What positive things are you going to begin to place into the universe daily?

_____

_____

_____

_____

_____

_____

_____

_____

_____

_____

_____

Good Morning...

You should want more for yourself with each new day that passes. Better your mind, body, and soul daily so no one can ever catch you slipping. It is all about self-love. Love starts with you.

What does your self-love journey look like to you?

_____

_____

_____

_____

_____

_____

_____

_____

_____

_____

_____

Good Morning...

You are worth more than what money can buy. You are more valued than you can ever imagine. Live for more than what the eyes can see, for the heart knows so much more.

What do you feel is worth more than money?

_____

_____

_____

_____

_____

_____

_____

_____

_____

_____

Good Morning…

Once you learn the secret to life, there will be no stopping you. With love, you have the capability to do all things. Do more things in love and watch your possibilities become endless.

How do you want to experience true love?

_____

_____

_____

_____

_____

_____

_____

_____

_____

_____

Good Morning...

Be ready for what the day has in store for you. Prevent it from having any effect on you negatively, for you are in control.

What are your triggers in life?

_____

_____

_____

_____

_____

_____

_____

_____

_____

_____

_____

_____

_____

Good Morning...

Acceptance is key. We might not agree on the same things, look the same, or even behave the same way, but that should never change the respect one has for themselves.

How do you respect yourself?

_____

_____

_____

_____

_____

_____

_____

_____

_____

_____

Good Morning...

Be true to yourself without people's influences, for that's what makes you unique.

What does being true to yourself look like for you?

_____

_____

_____

_____

_____

_____

_____

_____

_____

_____

_____

Good Morning...

Life may not be how you imagined it, but never lose hope. Even if you feel like you have nothing, someone out there is praying for what you have already.

What have you been wanting or needing to make your life feel more fulfilled?

_____

_____

_____

_____

_____

_____

_____

_____

_____

_____

_____

_____

Good Morning...

Do not let the chains of the world bring you down. What better way to live than to live freely.

What makes you come alive?

_____

_____

_____

_____

_____

_____

_____

_____

_____

_____

_____

Good Morning…

If love had a face, it would be represented by you, for you are the perfect example of what love looks like.

When you look in the mirror, what do you see and feel?

_____

_____

_____

_____

_____

_____

_____

_____

_____

_____

_____

_____

Good Morning...

Count your blessings and forget about the chaos. You are worth more than the misery in the universe, so always live above it.

What blessings do you currently have in your life?

_____

_____

_____

_____

_____

_____

_____

_____

_____

_____

_____

_____

Good Morning...

Push through the hardships with your head high knowing you hold the power. Never fold. Always find the next step to your plan.

What are your reasons for never giving up?

_____

_____

_____

_____

_____

_____

_____

_____

_____

_____

_____

_____

Good Morning…

If you knew that tomorrow was your last, would you be happy with the life you lived? If your answer is no, make a change starting today, for it is unhealthy to live a life you are not proud of.

What does a healthy life mean to you? Do you consider yourself to be living one?

_____

_____

_____

_____

_____

_____

_____

_____

_____

_____

_____

_____

Good Morning...

Never let situations or circumstances dictate your mood. Control it with a smile, as there is power behind your smile.

How much control do you have over your emotions?

_____

_____

_____

_____

_____

_____

_____

_____

_____

_____

_____

_____

_____

Good Morning...

Love yourself enough to know what is meant for you and what is not.
Forcing things into existence sets you up for failure. Let things happen
naturally and you will forever be truly living.

Why is it so hard to let go?

_____

_____

_____

_____

_____

_____

_____

_____

_____

_____

Good Morning...

When you feel like giving up, just think of all the reasons you are still standing. You are only given tough times because you have the endurance to handle them. Just search deep within for the strength. I know you will find it.

Where does your strength come from?

_____

_____

_____

_____

_____

_____

_____

_____

_____

_____

Good Morning...

You are an extraordinarily amazing person with assets that could benefit the world. If anyone tells you otherwise, just smile proving them wrong every time.

What assets do you bring to any table?

_____

_____

_____

_____

_____

_____

_____

_____

_____

_____

_____

Good Morning…

In a world filled with negativity and bitterness, be the individual to stand above all knowing we all were created for something greater.

What is your something better?

_____

_____

_____

_____

_____

_____

_____

_____

_____

_____

_____

_____

Good Morning...

The love you give is a representation of the love you are willing to receive. Open your heart in knowing all other things come to those who love.

What causes you to close off your heart?

_____

_____

_____

_____

_____

_____

_____

_____

_____

_____

_____

Good Morning...

The world is always going to throw curve balls your way. It is the ability to handle the curves that makes the difference.

What curve balls have you been faced with recently? How are you going to overcome them?

_____

_____

_____

_____

_____

_____

_____

_____

_____

_____

Good Morning…

Setting expectations only leads to heartaches and headaches. Do not expect anything and you will receive more than your heart's desires.

What has caused you heartache?

_____

_____

_____

_____

_____

_____

_____

_____

_____

_____

_____

_____

Good Morning...

Letting someone else's negativity latch onto you is like poison. It is time we detached ourselves from these individuals to live a more joyful life.

Who do you need to detach from in this life and why?

_____

_____

_____

_____

_____

_____

_____

_____

_____

_____

Good Morning…

The life you once lived does not represent who you are today. Stop being ridiculed by your past and create an even better future ahead. You deserve it.

What part of your past still controls you today?

_____

_____

_____

_____

_____

_____

_____

_____

_____

_____

_____

Good Morning...

We only take what we believe we are worth in life. See more in yourself and take action for a better tomorrow.

What do you see in yourself?

_____

_____

_____

_____

_____

_____

_____

_____

_____

_____

_____

_____

_____

Good Morning...

Get rid of the toxins that have been decreasing your growth and hold on to the things that bring you life. This journey is always better when you are enjoying life.

Name all the toxins in your life.

_____

_____

_____

_____

_____

_____

_____

_____

_____

_____

_____

Good Morning…

Spend your days loving all the things and people that keep you grounded. Letting society dictate how or what you should love does not allow you to experience what true happiness consists of.

Who or what keeps you grounded?

_____

_____

_____

_____

_____

_____

_____

_____

_____

_____

_____

_____

Good Morning...

Get rid of the toxins that have been decreasing your growth and hold on to the things that bring you life. This journey is always better when you are enjoying life.

Name all the toxins in your life.

_____

_____

_____

_____

_____

_____

_____

_____

_____

_____

Good Morning…

Spend your days loving all the things and people that keep you grounded. Letting society dictate how or what you should love does not allow you to experience what true happiness consists of.

Who or what keeps you grounded?

_____

_____

_____

_____

_____

_____

_____

_____

_____

_____

_____

Good Morning...

Struggling means there is a major lesson to be learned. Find the positivity in the struggle to watch yourself blossom.

Who are you blossoming into?

_____

_____

_____

_____

_____

_____

_____

_____

_____

_____

_____

_____

Good Morning...

Take a moment to welcome love, creativity, and good fortune into your life by aligning yourself in a way to receive. The lies in your mind are not true. You are capable of all things. Now is the time to believe it.

What have you been welcoming into your life recently?

_____

_____

_____

_____

_____

_____

_____

_____

_____

_____

_____

_____

Good Morning...

Break the chains that have held you back and have the confidence knowing you were created to experience the unthinkable.

How much confidence do you have in yourself?

_____

_____

_____

_____

_____

_____

_____

_____

_____

_____

_____

_____

Good Morning...

Growing as a person means having the ability to accept an apology that was never given. Do not let yourself stay stuck because of the actions or words of others. Forgive and move on, for there is so much more to life.

What makes forgiveness hard to do?

_____

_____

_____

_____

_____

_____

_____

_____

_____

_____

_____

Good Morning...

Time does not wait for anyone, so live each moment to the fullest knowing life is so much better when you are having fun.

What brings fun into your life?

_____

_____

_____

_____

_____

_____

_____

_____

_____

_____

_____

Good Morning...

You only have one life to live, so take chances and follow your heart. Fearing the unknown does not let the true you to flourish.

What are your innermost fears?

_____

_____

_____

_____

_____

_____

_____

_____

_____

_____

_____

_____

Good Morning...

To manifest the life of your dreams, you must let go of fear and embrace love. That is when you begin to tap into your full abundance.

How is abundance represented in your life?

_____

_____

_____

_____

_____

_____

_____

_____

_____

_____

_____

_____

_____

Good Morning…

Remember, at any given time, you can press the "reset" button allowing your true self to shine. You have the right to live and be free. Look within yourself.

How does your light shine in this world?

_____

_____

_____

_____

_____

_____

_____

_____

_____

_____

_____

_____

Good Morning…

Wake up refreshed, renewed, and reenergized. Be ready for what the universe has in store for you daily.

What energizes you and brings you so much life? Do you practice these things often?

Good Morning...

Your journey through this place called "life" will be one hell of a ride. Always remember you are worth every moment of clarity and positivity it has to offer you.

What clarity are you currently seeking in life?

_____

_____

_____

_____

_____

_____

_____

_____

_____

_____

_____

_____

_____

Good Morning...

When something is real, you will never have to fight for it. It just happens naturally. Hold on to the real people in your life, for holding on to the wrong ones can cause a life full of destruction.

Who do you consider to be the real people that have helped you grow in life?

_____

_____

_____

_____

_____

_____

_____

_____

_____

_____

Good Morning…

Wake each day with positivity on your mind and love in your heart. The world will always try to take control of your happiness. Why give them any reason to?

What are some judgments you have placed on yourself recently?

_____

_____

_____

_____

_____

_____

_____

_____

_____

_____

_____

_____

Good Morning...

When life does not seem to be going how you imagined, understand that there is something even greater on its way just for you. Just be patient.

What causes you to lack patience?

_____

_____

_____

_____

_____

_____

_____

_____

_____

_____

_____

Good Morning...

You were created to stand out from the rest; molded perfectly without any mistakes.

Why do you allow yourself to continue to relive mistakes you have already paid for?

_____

_____

_____

_____

_____

_____

_____

_____

_____

_____

_____

_____

Good Morning...

Never stop pursuing what you desire most in life, for living with regrets does not allow you to reach your full potential.

What regrets in life do you live with? What steps are you going to take to let them go?

_____

_____

_____

_____

_____

_____

_____

_____

_____

_____

_____

Good Morning...

Never be scared to say how you feel or speak up for yourself, for nothing gets accomplished with fear involved.

What causes you not to express your emotions or feelings when things are bothering you?

_____

_____

_____

_____

_____

_____

_____

_____

_____

_____

_____

_____

Good Morning...

You were meant to shine, so stop letting mediocrity and negativity dim your light.

Take a moment to write all the positive things going on in your life.

_____

_____

_____

_____

_____

_____

_____

_____

_____

_____

_____

_____

_____

Good Morning…

Be good to those that surround you. That love you. That accept you for who you are. We all need love to grow. We all deserve to be happy. More compassion… less judgement. It is the only way.

Do you trust yourself? Why or why not?

_____

_____

_____

_____

_____

_____

_____

_____

_____

_____

_____

_____

Good Morning...

When things seem to become complicated or start to not make sense, understand that your blessing is still coming. The chaos will subside and you will see the beauty unfold before your very eyes. Just have patience and believe.

What is complicated in your life that you have been trying to figure out? Take this space to dig deeper into it.

_____

_____

_____

_____

_____

_____

_____

_____

_____

_____

_____

Good Morning...

No one has the capability to take away the greatness that is inside of you. It is who you are. Have faith in your abilities and know you are truly unstoppable.

What do you believe you are capable of?

_____

_____

_____

_____

_____

_____

_____

_____

_____

_____

_____

_____

Good Morning...

We all expect life to go a certain way, when in reality life is a beautiful mystery unfolding before our very eyes. Embrace the unknown and make it your own.

What causes fear to play a factor in your life?

_____

_____

_____

_____

_____

_____

_____

_____

_____

_____

_____

Good Morning...

Remember to love in all circumstances or situations that occur during your lifetime, for love truly defeats all.

How is love viewed or measured in your opinion?

_____

_____

_____

_____

_____

_____

_____

_____

_____

_____

_____

_____

_____

Good Morning...

Always go for what you believe in, for regret is created when fear holds you back.

What parts of your life do you regret as a result of fear holding you back? What are you willing to do to change that?

_____

_____

_____

_____

_____

_____

_____

_____

_____

_____

_____

Good Morning...

Your mistakes have as much control over you as you allow them. Do not focus on them. Rather learn from them understanding that time is precious and cannot be gained back.

Name everything you wish to accomplish in life.

_____

_____

_____

_____

_____

_____

_____

_____

_____

_____

Good Morning...

Each day, someone or something is out to steal your joy. Will you continue to let these things have control over you or will you continue knowing you are given this life for mighty reasons? The choice is up to you.

Do you choose joy over all things in life? Why or why not?

_____

_____

_____

_____

_____

_____

_____

_____

_____

_____

_____

_____

Good Morning...

When everything seems to fail, keep pushing, for at times you must take life into your hands to create your own fairy tale.

How would you describe your own fairy tale?

_____

_____

_____

_____

_____

_____

_____

_____

_____

_____

_____

_____

_____

Good Morning...

Never stop reaching for your goals, for the light at the end of the tunnel is real. Keep pushing and believing, for the blessing is right ahead.

Name five blessings you received this past year.

_____

_____

_____

_____

_____

_____

_____

_____

_____

_____

_____

_____

Good Morning...

When life gets tough, search deep in your heart as to the true source of your happiness. Use that as motivation to reach the impossible.

What is your motivation in life?

_____

_____

_____

_____

_____

_____

_____

_____

_____

_____

_____

_____

Good Morning...

As you open your eyes and start your day, let it be done with love in your heart, for love outweighs any hatred.

What are your love languages?

_____

_____

_____

_____

_____

_____

_____

_____

_____

_____

_____

_____

Good Morning...

The time is now to make a difference in your life and in the lives of others. Stop waiting for the moment to approach to make changes. Approach the moment with great ideas knowing you were intended for great things.

What great things were you intended for?

_____

_____

_____

_____

_____

_____

_____

_____

_____

_____

_____

_____

Good Morning...

As humans, unconsciously, we find ourselves in circumstances in which we are at times unable to visualize a way out. I am here to remind you that there is always a way out.

When will you realize there is a solution to every circumstance? When will you believe you have greatness inside of you?

_____

_____

_____

_____

_____

_____

_____

_____

_____

_____

_____

_____

Good Morning...

Throughout life, we may find ourselves being taken advantage of, but never allow that to change the amazing person you are. Pivot yourself in a way that does not allow that to no longer happen. You know what to do!

What pivots should you be making in life right now?

_____

_____

_____

_____

_____

_____

_____

_____

_____

_____

_____

_____

Good Morning...

As you become one with yourself, you begin to unlock doors to endless possibilities. You have found your flow in life and it is so beautiful to watch. You are blossoming into one beautiful masterpiece. Trust your abilities.

What kind of masterpiece are you?

_____

_____

_____

_____

_____

_____

_____

_____

_____

_____

_____

_____

Good Morning...

Pain is a part of our lives, as it demands to be felt. Allow yourself to feel, but never let your pain blind you from the true peace that's on its way.

What type of inner peace do you desire to achieve in this lifetime?

_____

_____

_____

_____

_____

_____

_____

_____

_____

_____

_____

_____

_____

Good Morning...

Do things out of the kindness of your heart, not to receive things in return. In these moments, real blessings exist.

How are you practicing kindness towards yourself daily?

_____

_____

_____

_____

_____

_____

_____

_____

_____

_____

_____

Good Morning…

When your mind is racing and your heart is heavy, fear no more. Love yourself in those moments to eliminate what does not serve you.

What needs to be eliminated from your life that no longer serves you?

_____

_____

_____

_____

_____

_____

_____

_____

_____

_____

_____

_____

Good morning...

We as individuals become so self-consumed that we forget there is a bigger world out there; much greater. Free your mind, body, and soul, for your life means more than what society has to offer.

What does your life mean to you?

_____

_____

_____

_____

_____

_____

_____

_____

_____

_____

_____

Good Morning...

As the world continues to change and lives continue to be taken daily, take time to cherish priceless moments, memories, and people, for within seconds your life can be changed drastically.

What do you cherish most in life?

_____

_____

_____

_____

_____

_____

_____

_____

_____

_____

_____

_____

Good Morning...

Have you allowed your past to affect you by crippling you from life or have you allowed those moments to shape the dynamic person you are today? Only you can answer that question. We have the choice daily to choose which path we are willing to take. I pray you choose more for your life today and every day.

What would your inner child say to you today?

_____

_____

_____

_____

_____

_____

_____

_____

_____

_____

_____

Good Morning...

Each day provided is a reminder that you are destined for greatness. Take advantage of this opportunity, for many amongst us are lost looking for our way out.

What do you believe you are destined for?

_____

_____

_____

_____

_____

_____

_____

_____

_____

_____

_____

_____

Good Morning...

If no one told you today, let me be the first to say you are amazing. Continue to let the real you shine, as you are worthy, deserving, and enough.

What do you deserve in life?

_____

_____

_____

_____

_____

_____

_____

_____

_____

_____

_____

Good Morning…

Love with an open heart without any restrictions, for you have been loved unconditionally since the day you were born, whether you believe it or not.

What does love without restriction mean to your life?

_____

_____

_____

_____

_____

_____

_____

_____

_____

_____

_____

_____

Good Morning…

The amount of determination you have placed into yourself is out of this world. You inspire people without even knowing. You motivate people in ways that allow their best self to shine. Question is, are you giving that same love to yourself.

What are you going to do today to love yourself more?

_____

_____

_____

_____

_____

_____

_____

_____

_____

_____

_____

Good Morning...

Never lessen your value at the expense of others. Your life has so much meaning. Keep your head up at all times knowing the light always comes after darkness. All your uncertainties will soon be answered.

What uncertainties are you having about yourself?

_____

_____

_____

_____

_____

_____

_____

_____

_____

_____

_____

_____

Good Morning...

Live life like there is no tomorrow, for life is everything you make it.

If there was no tomorrow, how would you live your last day?

_____

_____

_____

_____

_____

_____

_____

_____

_____

_____

_____

_____

Good Morning...

It is time to enjoy every bit and piece of you. It is time to take off all the layers of fear, worry, and doubt replacing them with love, happiness, and success. It is the recipe to a good life.

What is your recipe for living a life of happiness, love, and success?

_____

_____

_____

_____

_____

_____

_____

_____

_____

_____

_____

_____

Good Morning…

You have a heart of gold and the endurance of a lion. There is no stopping you now. You have been placing nothing but goodness into this world and it shows. It is only right that it comes back to you.

What goodness have you been placing into the universe?

_____

_____

_____

_____

_____

_____

_____

_____

_____

_____

_____

Good Morning...

As individuals, we are never satisfied. Always looking in the mirror and not being fully happy with what we see. In these moments, do not let yourself become your own worst critic. Major growth comes with self-love. Love yourself first!

Take this space to speak about how happy you are with the person you are becoming.

_____

_____

_____

_____

_____

_____

_____

_____

_____

_____

_____

Good Morning...

You hold your value right inside of you. Never give anyone the opportunity to unbid your worth, for you, my dear, are more precious than life itself.

How much do you value yourself?

Good Morning…

Surround yourself with positivity, for negativity has a way of destroying lives without much effort.

How has negativity and misery affected your life?

_____

_____

_____

_____

_____

_____

_____

_____

_____

_____

_____

_____

_____

Good Morning...

Society teaches us to hate ourselves causing shame to be a part of our everyday living. Every part of us was carefully created in such remarkable ways. Self-love comes with an unlimited amount of strength. Tap into it daily.

How does body shaming play a part in your life? Are you happy with your body? Why or why not?

_____

_____

_____

_____

_____

_____

_____

_____

_____

_____

_____

Good Morning...

Even when the darkness takes over, do not feel defeated. Your darkness is your guide to your light, for you are victorious in all that you do.

What darkness did you face to get to your light?

_____

_____

_____

_____

_____

_____

_____

_____

_____

_____

_____

_____

_____

Good Morning...

Why wait for change to occur when you have the ability to change the world right inside of you?

How would you change the world if given the ability to?

_____

_____

_____

_____

_____

_____

_____

_____

_____

_____

_____

_____

Good Morning...

We are not obligated to stay the same. With each new chapter in our lives comes growth allowing us to flourish. Your happiness is very important in this life. There is no such thing as selfishness if it brings you happiness.

How do you need to be more selfish with your time to feed your soul?

_____

_____

_____

_____

_____

_____

_____

_____

_____

_____

_____

_____

Good Morning...

Not every day is going to be a positive day. Not every day will be a good day, but there is a reason to smile every day. Find the simple things in life and hold on to them, for you should never deny yourself the right to feel.

What simple things bring you the most bliss in life?

_____

_____

_____

_____

_____

_____

_____

_____

_____

_____

_____

Good Morning…

Follow your heart, for true love and happiness can never be replaced.

What does your heart say right now?

_____

_____

_____

_____

_____

_____

_____

_____

_____

_____

_____

_____

_____

Good Morning...

It is time we stopped taking short cuts while trying to create a life of fulfillment. Life has more meaning when you trust your process and have faith within yourself.

What does a fulfilled life look like to you?

_____

_____

_____

_____

_____

_____

_____

_____

_____

_____

_____

_____

Good Morning…

As humans, we strive for perfection not realizing that imperfections help us stand out from the rest. Be different. Be YOU.

How do you stand out from the rest?

_____

_____

_____

_____

_____

_____

_____

_____

_____

_____

_____

_____

_____

Good Morning...

Be thankful you were able to open your eyes to see a new day. A grateful heart is always the perfect start.

What is the first thing you thought of when you opened your eyes this morning? Is it something to be grateful for?

_____

_____

_____

_____

_____

_____

_____

_____

_____

_____

_____

Good Morning...

As humans, we get so caught up with our normal routines that we tend to miss out on the best moments in life.

What would you consider to be the best moment in your life and why?

_____

_____

_____

_____

_____

_____

_____

_____

_____

_____

_____

_____

_____

Good Morning...

Treat others how you would want to be treated, for at times we take advantage of people without realizing it. The time is now to make this change, for there could be no tomorrow.

How do you desire to be treated?

_____

_____

_____

_____

_____

_____

_____

_____

_____

_____

_____

Good Morning...

Life is not to be lived miserably, rather one of happiness, as life lessons are created to help us. The ability to overcome life's hardest challenges makes you who you are today.

What challenges have you overcome?

_____

_____

_____

_____

_____

_____

_____

_____

_____

_____

_____

_____

Good Morning...

This day wasn't given to make excuses, but to create productivity. Make the most out of your time, for any moment given can be taken.

How are you going to be more productive today?

_____

_____

_____

_____

_____

_____

_____

_____

_____

_____

_____

_____

_____

Good Morning...

Blessed are those that embrace each day to the fullest. We are ever changing, evolving, and coming into our true self. Do not place any more pressures onto being yourself.

Do you like your true self? Why or why not?

_____

_____

_____

_____

_____

_____

_____

_____

_____

_____

_____

_____

Good Morning…

With love, all things are possible. Continue doing what you love, and you will never have the need for anything else, for love withholds the test of times.

Create a list of all the things you like to do to love yourself more.

_____

_____

_____

_____

_____

_____

_____

_____

_____

_____

_____

Good Morning...

You were amazingly created with endless possibilities at your fingertips. Stop allowing time to pass you by and take advantage of the opportunity given, for someone out there is wishing they were you.

What causes doubt in your life?

_____

_____

_____

_____

_____

_____

_____

_____

_____

_____

_____

_____

Good Morning…

You are worthy of all the amazing things life has to offer, but do not forget the true miracle is within the struggle.

What struggles are you faced with today?

_____

_____

_____

_____

_____

_____

_____

_____

_____

_____

_____

_____

Good Morning...

The roadblocks in life are just reminders that something better lies ahead, so stay positive with your head high, for life will always have a way to surprise you.

How has life surprised you recently?

_____

_____

_____

_____

_____

_____

_____

_____

_____

_____

_____

_____

_____

Good Morning...

Be inspired by the things that surround you daily, for when we embrace adversity, we will be able to achieve the unthinkable.

What is the unthinkable you are trying to achieve?

_____

_____

_____

_____

_____

_____

_____

_____

_____

_____

_____

_____

Good Morning…

Be grateful/thankful for the life you have been provided, for each person's story should not be compared to the next persons. We've all been given our lives for a purpose, so take the good with the bad and keep striving for excellence.

What does excellence look like to you?

_____

_____

_____

_____

_____

_____

_____

_____

_____

_____

_____

_____

_____

Good Morning…

Treat each new day as an opportunity for growth. You may not be where you would like, but don't ever let that discourage you, for hardships separate the weak from the strong. Which one are you?

Would you consider yourself weak or strong? Why?

_____

_____

_____

_____

_____

_____

_____

_____

_____

_____

_____

Good Morning...

Never be ashamed of the sacrifices you have had to make to create a better future. For everyone speaks of a new life, but many find themselves stuck in their ways unable to make progress. Be amongst the ones that keep going.

What is your life plan? Take this time to write out the steps to be clear with your vision

_____

_____

_____

_____

_____

_____

_____

_____

_____

_____

_____

_____

Good Morning...

You have two choices in life: either keep pushing or give up, for life does not wait for anyone, and the strongest individuals can always go a little more.

What little more do you have left to give to yourself today?

_____

_____

_____

_____

_____

_____

_____

_____

_____

_____

Good Morning...

If life decides to take a different path than you expected, there's no reason to panic. Remain calm and patient. Life always has a way of preparing you for something even greater.

How do display patience towards your own self?

_____

_____

_____

_____

_____

_____

_____

_____

_____

_____

_____

_____

Good Morning...

Pain is a reminder that you are alive. Take the good with the bad, for pain is something that needs to be felt to overcome.

What has caused some type of pain recently? Describe the way it made you feel and how you will move through it.

_____

_____

_____

_____

_____

_____

_____

_____

_____

_____

_____

_____

Good Morning...

Activate your favor by believing in the power of just being you. It is your birthright to receive blessings.

What do you believe are your birthrights?

_____

_____

_____

_____

_____

_____

_____

_____

_____

_____

_____

_____

_____

Good Morning...

Just when you thought life could not get any better... TODAY
arrived.
There are breakthroughs with your name written all over them.
Choose today to believe in the magic inside of you.

What breakthrough have you been waiting for?

_____

_____

_____

_____

_____

_____

_____

_____

_____

_____

_____

_____

Good Morning...

The worries of the world are not your problem. The outer world will always try to disturb your inner peace. Be strong enough to know what you built inside of you cannot be shaken. You are covered and protected.

What worries are on your heart today?

_____

_____

_____

_____

_____

_____

_____

_____

_____

_____

_____

Good Morning…

Create the world you desire to live in around you. Allow your energy to flow without judgement or demand. Keep an open heart to attract the abundance that is yours.

What are you currently trying to attract in your life?

_____

_____

_____

_____

_____

_____

_____

_____

_____

_____

_____

Good Morning...

When all else fails and you feel like your world is crumbling, just hold on, for the strong will always survive.

What are your strengths and weaknesses?

_____

_____

_____

_____

_____

_____

_____

_____

_____

_____

_____

_____

Good Morning...

Live life to the fullest without the approval of others, for your happiness may not reflect the happiness of others.

Name all the things that effect your happiness.

_____

_____

_____

_____

_____

_____

_____

_____

_____

_____

_____

_____

_____

Good Morning…

Thoughts have energy, so make sure to always keep your head in a safe place. Bad days will come upon us, but allow yourself to continuously flow through the chaos. No damage can be done on your beautiful spirit. Trust yourself more to know you are healing.

What is your spirit saying to you today?

_____

_____

_____

_____

_____

_____

_____

_____

_____

_____

_____

_____

Good Morning...

Some people are meant to be in your life for a season, while others are meant to impact your life for a reason. Be aware of the differences, for temporary people should never have permanent effects on your life.

What are your boundaries?

_____

_____

_____

_____

_____

_____

_____

_____

_____

_____

_____

Good Morning...

Do not seek approval, for your life was already approved when you were sent here. You are validated and enough, for even in chaos there is beauty.

What beauty have you found within your struggle?

_____

_____

_____

_____

_____

_____

_____

_____

_____

_____

_____

Good Morning...

Life is one big adventure, so dive in head first, for you only regret moments that are not taken.

What has been causing you to second-guess yourself recently?

_____

_____

_____

_____

_____

_____

_____

_____

_____

_____

_____

_____

_____

Good Morning...

Your future is bright, and your past is how you got here. Continue this path called LIFE knowing what was meant to break you never did.

Does your past hinder your present? Why or why not? If so, how will you make the change to live differently?

_____

_____

_____

_____

_____

_____

_____

_____

_____

_____

_____

_____

_____

Good Morning...

Do not be afraid to take chances. As one door closes, another door opens, so live life knowing something better is in store for you.

What does something better look like to you?

_____

_____

_____

_____

_____

_____

_____

_____

_____

_____

_____

_____

_____

Good Morning...

Your mental health is important and always should be put first. Never give up the good fight knowing you are worth it. Understand that it may take some dark days to reach the light, but everything you are going through will make sense soon. Just hold on.

What is your mental health status at the moment?

_____

_____

_____

_____

_____

_____

_____

_____

_____

_____

_____

_____

Good Morning...

When life decides to take you down a different path, embrace it, for life is consistently changing and you must learn how to pivot to make it in this world.

What different path have you been taken down recently?

_____

_____

_____

_____

_____

_____

_____

_____

_____

_____

_____

_____

Good Morning...

When life gets hard, find the peace inside to not allow your mind to be corrupted by the negativity. Your mind is a sacred place that should never be compromised.

Describe the peace inside of you to help you through the tough times. If you do not have peace inside, describe the peace you desire.

_____

_____

_____

_____

_____

_____

_____

_____

_____

_____

_____

Good Morning...

Take a few minutes out of your day to commend yourself for being the amazing person you are. Many people are still lost placing energy into things of the world instead of taking care of themselves. Which one are you?

What worldly things do you consume yourself with? Is it adding value to your life?

_____

_____

_____

_____

_____

_____

_____

_____

_____

_____

_____

Good Morning...

The life you live is one you believe, see, and feel. The winners in life only win because they believe in themselves wholeheartedly.

Question is, are you doing the same? Why or why not?

_____

_____

_____

_____

_____

_____

_____

_____

_____

_____

_____

_____

Good Morning...

We all were created beautifully with flaws and imperfections. Embrace those parts of you knowing they set you apart from the rest. You are enough and deserving of living a great life. Problem is, you may not believe it.

What makes you believe you are not good enough or deserving of living a better life?

_____

_____

_____

_____

_____

_____

_____

_____

_____

_____

Good Morning…

Believe in yourself. Love yourself. Invest in yourself and watch how the universe makes your dream your reality.

What reality are you currently living?

_____

_____

_____

_____

_____

_____

_____

_____

_____

_____

_____

_____

Good Morning...

Your future self is so proud of all the progression you have been making. You have been placing in the work for a better future. You've been taking the harder road in life knowing it will lead you to beautiful rewards. You haven't given up on yourself. That alone is beautiful.

What motivates you?

_____

_____

_____

_____

_____

_____

_____

_____

_____

_____

_____

_____

Good Morning…

You should always feel amazing when choosing yourself first. For so long, you have placed so much of your dream on the back burner that now is your time. Let your light shine and never dim again for anyone or anything.

What makes you feel amazing?

_____

_____

_____

_____

_____

_____

_____

_____

_____

_____

_____

_____

Good Morning...

The mask we painted on our face is not the face of our hearts. Be true to who you are without fear, worry, doubt, or shame, for you are a remarkable person made with LOVE.

What mask do you paint on your face daily? Does your mask change depending on who you are with?

_____

_____

_____

_____

_____

_____

_____

_____

_____

_____

_____

Good Morning...

Never forget one must pay a price or sacrifice in life to secure one's blessings. Nothing in this world comes easy, but in the end it is all worth it.

What prices have you paid to live a better life?

_____

_____

_____

_____

_____

_____

_____

_____

_____

_____

_____

Good Morning…

Life is a beautiful adventure just waiting to be unfolded. Stop limiting yourself to what the world thinks is happiness, for you deserve the world and more. Live in your own happiness.

What adventure are you currently on?

_____

_____

_____

_____

_____

_____

_____

_____

_____

_____

_____

_____

Good Morning...

The mind is a terrible thing to waste and such an amazing thing to possess. Life becomes even more difficult when you let negative thoughts and feelings fester. It is time to renew your mind, body, and soul daily to allow yourself to experience true freedom.

What has your mind been telling you recently?

_____

_____

_____

_____

_____

_____

_____

_____

_____

_____

_____

Good Morning…

Live each day doing what you love. If you do not love, you are not living.

If life had no restrictions, how would you live your life?

_____

_____

_____

_____

_____

_____

_____

_____

_____

_____

_____

_____

_____

Good Morning...

Never feel bad for the decisions you have made. Life should be lived with no regrets. Allow yourself to grow and always remember lessons learned is wisdom earned.

Name some lessons you have learned that have allowed your wisdom to grow.

_____

_____

_____

_____

_____

_____

_____

_____

_____

_____

_____

_____

Good Morning…

Letting temporary people have permanent places in your heart leaves room for poison festering in your life. They do not deserve your presence, for your energy is worth so much more.

Why is it hard to let go of people you know are not good for you?

_____

_____

_____

_____

_____

_____

_____

_____

_____

_____

_____

_____

Good Morning…

Take a moment for yourself. Be good to yourself and treat yourself well. For love starts with self and stems into every relationship we ever encounter.

How well do you treat yourself?

_____

_____

_____

_____

_____

_____

_____

_____

_____

_____

_____

Good Morning...

The power needed to change your life in dynamic ways is right inside of you. Stop waiting for a moment to arrive and take your life back. You are braver and stronger than life's toughest battles. Don't you believe it?

Do you believe you have power? Why or why not?

_____

_____

_____

_____

_____

_____

_____

_____

_____

_____

_____

_____

Good Morning...

What matters most is how you feel about yourself without the opinions and actions of others being a contributing factor. You should never have to question the goodness of your heart.

What does your heart say about you?

_____

_____

_____

_____

_____

_____

_____

_____

_____

_____

_____

_____

Good Morning...

When was the last time you told yourself "I love you?" Saying these three magical words to yourself can raise your vibration instantly. Make it a habit to show yourself love daily knowing with self-love you become unstoppable.

Do you make it a habit to say "I love you" daily to yourself? Why or why not? How does it make you feel?

_____

_____

_____

_____

_____

_____

_____

_____

_____

_____

Good Morning…

Possibilities are endless when you open your mind, body, and soul. Remaining closed off does not allow you to take steps forward. It, instead, keeps you stagnant never living your life to your full potential.

Are you adding darkness or light to this world and how?

_____

_____

_____

_____

_____

_____

_____

_____

_____

_____

_____

_____

Good Morning…

All the sweat, blood, and tears you have shed are all for a reason. They would never go in vain if you believe better times are near. They will lead to your greatness in the end.

What better times are you inspiring to have?

_____

_____

_____

_____

_____

_____

_____

_____

_____

_____

_____

Good Morning...

Never be ashamed of showing love in a society that teaches you otherwise. Love overcomes all things allowing one's soul to soar. Always stay true to who you are.

What makes your heart soar? Are you living that life today?

_____

_____

_____

_____

_____

_____

_____

_____

_____

_____

_____

Good Morning...

Start your day with a smile knowing you are one of a kind. No one could ever be YOU. You were amazingly created to achieve the impossible. You have the world in the palm of your hands. All it takes now is belief in self.

What is your interpretation of a smile?

_____

_____

_____

_____

_____

_____

_____

_____

_____

_____

_____

Good Morning…

Limiting yourself to what this society influences you to be is a no-go.
You were given this life to be extraordinary. Take advantage of what
it has to offer you knowing your life is aligned for astounding things.

How aligned have you been living recently?

_____

_____

_____

_____

_____

_____

_____

_____

_____

_____

_____

Good Morning...

Tomorrow is not promised, and you may never have a second chance. How you live today can determine the outcome of your future. Hope you decide to live a better life.

What are you going to start doing differently to live a more fulfilled life?

_____

_____

_____

_____

_____

_____

_____

_____

_____

_____

_____

_____

Good Morning...

If you want something, go after it without distractions or fear. Crippling yourself leads to a life of restrictions and limitations. Go get that best life you've always wanted.

Describe the last time you lived in fear and overcame it.

_____

_____

_____

_____

_____

_____

_____

_____

_____

_____

_____

_____

_____

Good Morning...

If something feels right, do it. Life is much more fulfilling when you do things out of the ordinary.

What would you like to accomplish in life that seems out of the ordinary?

_____

_____

_____

_____

_____

_____

_____

_____

_____

_____

_____

Good Morning...

The best moments in life come unexpectedly and leave such beautiful imprints on your heart. Embrace these moments to the fullest knowing we may not get this chance ever again in the world we live in today.

What unexpected moments do you value most?

_____

_____

_____

_____

_____

_____

_____

_____

_____

_____

_____

Good Morning...

Live outside the box, for living inside one requires uniformity in a world where you are supposed to be different.

What encourages you to live outside the box?

_____

_____

_____

_____

_____

_____

_____

_____

_____

_____

_____

Good Morning...

There is no better way to live life unless you are smiling, for a smile can change a person's perspective in an instant.

What is your perspective about life currently?

_____

_____

_____

_____

_____

_____

_____

_____

_____

_____

_____

Good Morning...

There's no better time than now to go after what your heart desires.
Stop waiting for the perfect moment. Your happiness awaits you.

What desires for change will you be placing into the world?

_____

_____

_____

_____

_____

_____

_____

_____

_____

_____

Good Morning...

Don't ever worry about what people think of you. You will never be good enough in life if you continue to live by others' expectations. It is your life. Live it by your rules.

Do the opinions of others effect the way you view yourself? Why or why not?

_____

_____

_____

_____

_____

_____

_____

_____

_____

_____

_____

Good Morning…

Love without restrictions and laugh to the temporary circumstances you are faced with daily. You are only given this opportunity at life once, so make the most of it. Show yourself how courageous you really are.

How do you make the most out of this life?

_____

_____

_____

_____

_____

_____

_____

_____

_____

_____

_____

_____

Good Morning...

When life tries to knock you down, stand tall knowing something better is in store. You were made for brilliance and no one can eliminate that power within you.

How has life been trying to knock you down recently?

_____

_____

_____

_____

_____

_____

_____

_____

_____

_____

_____

_____

Good Morning...

Take chances and never underestimate yourself, for the people who succeed know what it means to try time and time again.

How do you underestimate yourself at times?

_____

_____

_____

_____

_____

_____

_____

_____

_____

_____

_____

_____

Good Morning...

Continue being you, for the best people in life live outside of the expectation of others.

Who are you beyond the thoughts you have created about yourself?

_____

_____

_____

_____

_____

_____

_____

_____

_____

_____

_____

_____

Good Morning...

Never allow yourself to give up on something your heart desires. Many will fail, but the strong will always find their way out of the chaos.

What is something you gave up on that you still desire in life?

_____

_____

_____

_____

_____

_____

_____

_____

_____

_____

_____

Good Morning...

Throughout your day, take a few minutes to focus on yourself. Being selfish is not always a bad thing when it comes to your health and wellness. Fuel your body with what it needs to win any race.

How does your health and wellness add value to the beautiful life you are seeking?

_____

_____

_____

_____

_____

_____

_____

_____

_____

_____

_____

_____

Good Morning...

Be grateful for what you have, for any day it could be taken in a blink of an eye. Your life is meaningful and should be lived to the fullest.

Who or what would you miss most if tomorrow did not happen and why?

_____

_____

_____

_____

_____

_____

_____

_____

_____

_____

_____

Good morning...

When you least expect it, life could take a left or right turn, but that does not mean life is over. Find something positive in everything you encounter. It is all a part of your journey.

Do you believe there is room for more growth in your journey? In what ways?

_____

_____

_____

_____

_____

_____

_____

_____

_____

_____

_____

Good Morning...

When something real comes along, there is no reason to be afraid, for steps taken without fear result in everlasting happiness. You are worth it all.

What makes you fearless?

_____

_____

_____

_____

_____

_____

_____

_____

_____

_____

_____

Good Morning...

You may not have control over certain things that may have happened in your lifetime, but one thing you can control is whether your reaction betters or worsens your life. Make the right decision for your life starting today because a life without healing leaves too many disappointments.

What disappointments have you experienced in life that still bother you until this day?

_____

_____

_____

_____

_____

_____

_____

_____

_____

_____

Good Morning...

You are worthy more than you give yourself credit for, so pat yourself on the back. You made it this far and you will only make it farther. You are a miracle in progress.

Do you consider yourself to be a miracle in progress? Why or why not?

_____

_____

_____

_____

_____

_____

_____

_____

_____

_____

_____

Good Morning...

There comes a time in life when people decide to show their true colors to you. Take it for face value, for being blinded is not a positive way of learning in life.

What blinds you from seeing the true color in others?

_____

_____

_____

_____

_____

_____

_____

_____

_____

_____

_____

_____

Good Morning...

Embrace the unexpected moments of happiness when hardships become overwhelming in your life. Find that happy space that will provide you with the comfort and patience needed to handle the situation at hand.

What is your happy space? Describe how it makes you feel.

_____

_____

_____

_____

_____

_____

_____

_____

_____

_____

_____

_____

Good Morning...

Appreciate the little things in life, for they have a way of reminding you that you are always meant to feel special.

Do you currently feel special? Why or why not?

_____

_____

_____

_____

_____

_____

_____

_____

_____

_____

_____

Good Morning...

Love yourself more than any label, diagnoses, addiction, sickness, fear, or concept. Set yourself free and heal yourself with the most important love there is in this big world... YOURS!

What addiction are you currently faced with that is not adding value to your life? Remember, addiction can be a person, place, or thing. Addiction is not just drugs.

_____

_____

_____

_____

_____

_____

_____

_____

_____

_____

Good Morning...

Take it easy on yourself as you are trying your best during such times. Understand that focusing deeply on the real one who matters most is important. That real one is you.

Where has your focus been recently?

_____

_____

_____

_____

_____

_____

_____

_____

_____

_____

_____

Good Morning...

Embrace the true meaning of love as you accept the true meaning of being you. Love is our natural state and forever will be. Love is who we are. Never forget that.

What parts of yourself do you need to work on more?

_____

_____

_____

_____

_____

_____

_____

_____

_____

_____

_____

Good Morning…

Never allow anyone or anything to have power over YOU. Power comes from within. Tap into who you really are. That is how you find your ultimate strength.

How are you able to tap into your strength when you need it most?

_____

_____

_____

_____

_____

_____

_____

_____

_____

_____

_____

Good Morning...

As you awake this morning, be thankful for all you have. As humans, we get caught up in the "world" that we lose sight of our real priorities. Understand that no tangible item can be taken when it is your time to leave this earth, so why continue to allow it to have control over you while you are living?

Name the real priorities in your life.

_____

_____

_____

_____

_____

_____

_____

_____

_____

_____

_____

Good Morning…

You did it. You made it through another day, and for that you should be proud of yourself. All the hardships you experienced were all worth it, for they build character and strength.

When the light seems to be at the end of the tunnel, what keeps you optimistic about life?

_____

_____

_____

_____

_____

_____

_____

_____

_____

_____

_____

Good Morning...

At times, we do not give ourselves enough credit. We stare at the bigger picture wanting more, forgetting change happens one step at a time. Be proud of who you are becoming and have faith that with each step taken it will lead to an even brighter tomorrow.

Take this space to give yourself credit. To give yourself love without any structure given.

_____

_____

_____

_____

_____

_____

_____

_____

_____

_____

Good Morning…

When the times get rough or you feel you cannot go on any longer, search deep within yourself; the power is embedded right inside of you. You must find it!

What ultimate event helped you find your strength?

_____

_____

_____

_____

_____

_____

_____

_____

_____

_____

_____

_____

Good Morning...

When things happen unexpectedly, take it as a blessing to prevent you from continuing down the wrong path, rather than an obstacle you are faced with.

What causes you to take things personally?

_____

_____

_____

_____

_____

_____

_____

_____

_____

_____

_____

_____

Good Morning...

Today is meant for smiles and laughter. Many times, we get stuck without knowing whether to go left or right. It makes us frustrated due to lack of control. Stop allowing these moments to overwhelm you and just smile.

How do you regroup yourself after losing control?

_____

_____

_____

_____

_____

_____

_____

_____

_____

_____

_____

Good morning...

Never allow someone's negativity deter you from your dreams and goals, for it is your life to be lived. Stop giving people the power in your life when all the power you need is right inside of you. Believe in your abilities and have faith knowing you can complete the impossible

What is needed to turn your impossibilities into possibilities?

_____

_____

_____

_____

_____

_____

_____

_____

_____

_____

Good Morning...

May this day bring you positivity and growth, for negativity seems to be spreading miserably across the world. Do not allow yourself to be sucked into it either. Keep pushing forward knowing the end result will be worthwhile.

What keeps you fueled up during chaos?

_____

_____

_____

_____

_____

_____

_____

_____

_____

_____

_____

Good Morning…

Today is all about living in complete joy. You hold the power and never allow anyone to tell you otherwise. You were born to transform the world in beautiful ways. Believe in these abilities and take that first step. I promise you will not regret it.

When you don't feel in control, what coping methods do you or could you use to ground yourself?

_____

_____

_____

_____

_____

_____

_____

_____

_____

_____

_____

Good Morning...

You were uniquely made with endurance and drive to accomplish anything you put your mind to. You have strength that can last your whole lifetime. Allowing another minute to fly by is just a waste. Rise up knowing you are capable.

What makes you unique and capable?

_____

_____

_____

_____

_____

_____

_____

_____

_____

_____

_____

_____

Good Morning...

May this day bring your life strength, growth, positivity in a world consistently trying to pull you down. Discouragement, fear, and worry no longer exist in your world. Only lessons and love. Accept it all.

What makes it hard for you to accept love?

_____

_____

_____

_____

_____

_____

_____

_____

_____

_____

_____

_____

Good Morning...

Find that light in your life and continue to hold on, for every storm eventually clears. Do not allow the moment to confuse your mind. Rise up knowing love will always find a way.

What or who is the light of your life and why?

_____

_____

_____

_____

_____

_____

_____

_____

_____

_____

_____

Morning…

Take a second to reflect on all you've ever been through in life compared to where you are now. No one said life would be easy, but it is determination that makes one become successful.

How determined are you in life?

_____

_____

_____

_____

_____

_____

_____

_____

_____

_____

_____

Good Morning...

If no one has said it recently, I will: YOU'RE WONDERFULLY MADE JUST THE WAY YOU ARE. Learn to see it for yourself and cherish it, for tomorrow waits for no one.

What have you learned recently about yourself?

_____

_____

_____

_____

_____

_____

_____

_____

_____

_____

_____

Good Morning…

As the days seem to be going by quicker, take this opportunity to share the art of LOVE. Stop allowing yourself to dwell in the negative moments, for life is better when you are enjoying it.

How do you display the art of love in your life?

_____

_____

_____

_____

_____

_____

_____

_____

_____

_____

_____

_____

Good Morning...

Wake up appreciating what life has blessed you with daily. Stop comparing yourself to the next person or wishing for more, for your decisions have paved the way for your future. Appreciate all you have been given to receive even more in life.

How does appreciation play a role in your life?

_____

_____

_____

_____

_____

_____

_____

_____

_____

_____

_____

Good Morning...

You can overcome anything with positivity and perseverance. The need to get out of character lets you know what else you need to heal from. Do not be afraid to explore your own needs because when you are 100% the world appreciates you even more.

What role does perseverance play in your life?

_____

_____

_____

_____

_____

_____

_____

_____

_____

_____

_____

Good Morning…

In a world full of chaos, LOVE for yourself should always be your first answer. Anything less causes doubt, worry, and fear to make their way into your life.

What is so hard about loving yourself first?

_____

_____

_____

_____

_____

_____

_____

_____

_____

_____

_____

_____

Good Morning...

Never take a person for granted, for time waits for no one. Eliminate the arguments, learn to compromise, and appreciate every moment, for love is always the way out.

Who have you taken for granted recently? Is it you or others? Why has this happened?

_____

_____

_____

_____

_____

_____

_____

_____

_____

_____

_____

_____

Good Morning...

Everyone will know a different version of you, but the true you lie inside of you. Be true to the real you.

What makes you think differently than the way you feel in your heart?

_____

_____

_____

_____

_____

_____

_____

_____

_____

_____

Good Morning…

May you have awakened refreshed and ready to conquer life's toughest battles. No one said life would be easy, but it is the trails that build one's character.

How would you define your character?

_____

_____

_____

_____

_____

_____

_____

_____

_____

_____

_____

_____

Good morning...

Regardless of what pain your childhood has caused you, you were born to thrive in this lifetime. Find your courage and strength within to handle all life has to show you.

What childhood trauma do you still need to heal from?

_____

_____

_____

_____

_____

_____

_____

_____

_____

_____

_____

Good Morning...

You are bigger and better than any obstacle, challenge, or problem thrown your way. During these moments of uncertainty, keep pushing forward, for anything worth having is worth fighting for.

How much are you worth fighting for?

_____

_____

_____

_____

_____

_____

_____

_____

_____

_____

_____

_____

Good morning…

Be thankful for life. Remember, everything happens for a reason, even if the reason is unclear at that moment. Take the negative and transform it to positive, for your energy is too sacred to be wasted away.

How do you honor your energy daily?

_____

_____

_____

_____

_____

_____

_____

_____

_____

_____

_____

_____

Good Morning…

You are blessed beyond words can explain. You may not feel that way right now, but it is true. Change your perspective and the universe will smile back at you each time.

Describe the blessed world you live in regardless of the obstacles you are faced with.

_____

_____

_____

_____

_____

_____

_____

_____

_____

_____

_____

Good Morning...

You can only do as much as a person allows you to do. Best thing needed is prayer, for prayer works miracles in the lives of many.

What prayers are you sending into the universe as of today?

_____

_____

_____

_____

_____

_____

_____

_____

_____

_____

_____

_____

_____

Good Morning...

When it is raining, look at its beauty, for everything worth having comes with some type of hurdle.

What hurdles are you faced with presently?

_____

_____

_____

_____

_____

_____

_____

_____

_____

_____

_____

_____

Good Morning…

May you have awakened with a smile knowing you have been given another chance at this thing we call "life." You are bigger, better, and smarter than any barrier thrown your way. Keep rising to the top, for there is truly no limitation to happiness.

How are you doing at this thing called "LIFE?"

_____

_____

_____

_____

_____

_____

_____

_____

_____

_____

_____

Good Morning…

It is time to take matters into your own hands and create something magical, for those who are remembered are the ones that keep pushing, regardless of how hard life gets.

How has life made you or broken you?

_____

_____

_____

_____

_____

_____

_____

_____

_____

_____

_____

_____

Good Morning...

Forgiveness is essential to life. Without it, you live in binds separating you from truly living. Allow yourself to be free of any chain and let go of the emotions you once felt, for forgiveness is all about you, not anyone else.

Who is it you still need to forgive in this life? What has taken you so long to forgive the person?

_____

_____

_____

_____

_____

_____

_____

_____

_____

_____

Good Morning…

Life is like a roller coaster; it continues to have its highs and lows. The low moments are meant to teach a lesson, not to determine an individual's future. The lows do not last forever, as the highs will come faster if you just let go.

Describe the highs and lows in your life currently.

_____

_____

_____

_____

_____

_____

_____

_____

_____

_____

_____

Good Morning...

As your day progresses, take out the time to evaluate your life and understand what truly makes you happy. Those are your reasons for living. Choose to see the world differently with the ability to cherish each moment, for memories last a lifetime.

What awakens your heart?

_____

_____

_____

_____

_____

_____

_____

_____

_____

_____

_____

Good Morning...

As individuals, we get so stuck in our low moments that we forget the bigger picture ahead. Break all those chains and transform your life in dynamic ways. It is all setting you up for something greater.

What is the something greater you are setting yourself up for?

_____

_____

_____

_____

_____

_____

_____

_____

_____

_____

_____

Good Morning...

Feed yourself with the love and respect you deserve. Making your temple strong allows you to reach the best parts of who you are.

What is the best part of being you?

_____

_____

_____

_____

_____

_____

_____

_____

_____

_____

_____

Good Morning...

Stop saying the would-haves, should-haves, and could-haves and just do. You will never know what you can accomplish until you put your full effort to try.

What causes you to think you will fail?

_____

_____

_____

_____

_____

_____

_____

_____

_____

_____

_____

Good Morning...

Smiling is contagious, so make sure to spread the gift daily, for your smile can change the world in which you live in. Your smile is your birthright. Never lose it.

What gifts do you have to present to the world?

_____

_____

_____

_____

_____

_____

_____

_____

_____

_____

_____

_____

Good Morning...

The enemy was placed in our lives to rob and steal us of our joy. Regardless of the outcome, today, continue being you because good days only come to those who go after them.

How do you prevent the enemy from robbing and stealing your joy?

_____

_____

_____

_____

_____

_____

_____

_____

_____

_____

Good Morning...

As the day progresses, take time out to evaluate what truly provides your life with peace and tranquility, for those moments will outlast any storm you are faced with in life.

What can you do to bring tranquility to your life during any storm?

_____

_____

_____

_____

_____

_____

_____

_____

_____

_____

_____

_____

Good Morning…

Refuse to allow yourself to be consumed by society; dictating the way you should think or feel. Overcome all those barriers, for true happiness is found within.

Are you secure with the person you are today? What can you do to not allow the barriers to get in your way?

_____

_____

_____

_____

_____

_____

_____

_____

_____

_____

Good Morning...

As time progresses, start to realize all the beauty that surrounds you on a consistent basis. No one can see beauty through your eyes, but you. Allowing these different forms of media to tell you how to live will only take you farther away from the life you want to live.

Name all the beautiful things you have in your life.

_____

_____

_____

_____

_____

_____

_____

_____

_____

_____

_____

_____

Good Morning...

Throughout your day, take a second to be thankful for all you have been given, for living should never be unforgettable.

When you leave this world, what legacy do you want to leave behind?

_____

_____

_____

_____

_____

_____

_____

_____

_____

_____

_____

_____

Good Morning...

You will continue to be your worst critic if you allow it. There is no growth within a negative mindset causing you not to progress to your best.

What causes you to be so hard on yourself?

_____

_____

_____

_____

_____

_____

_____

_____

_____

_____

_____

_____

Good Morning...

Life is about exploring and inspiring; allowing yourself to not be denied by the factors of this world. Misery will always be around, but having your peace is all you need to make it far.

If you could explore the world doing what you love, where would you go and why?

Good Morning...

Life is designed to build strength, admiration, and character. Stop allowing temporary situations tell you how to feel, for your reaction reflects your growth.

How much have your grown since 1, 5, 10 years ago?

_____

_____

_____

_____

_____

_____

_____

_____

_____

_____

_____

_____

Good Morning...

Stay humble and continue moving forward, for your character determines your future.

What does being humble mean to you? Do you currently represent that in your life?

_____

_____

_____

_____

_____

_____

_____

_____

_____

_____

_____

_____

Good Morning...

Establishing an unbreakable connection these days appears to be a challenge but never impossible.When you find genuine individuals in your life, hold on to them, for your blessing might be standing right in front of you.

Describe the unbreakable connection that you yearn for.

_____

_____

_____

_____

_____

_____

_____

_____

_____

_____

_____

Good Morning…

It is our responsibility to build each other up with a humble mentality to spread love and continue pushing each other for a higher common goal: success. We all have a dream.

Do you consider yourself to be successful today? Why or why not? It's all about perspective, never forget that.

_____

_____

_____

_____

_____

_____

_____

_____

_____

_____

_____

Good Morning…

The peace needed to strive to greatness comes from the ability to forgive. Never allow yourself to be held down due to grudges or incidents that have occurred, for you deserve to live a life of bliss. Give it to yourself.

What do you need to forgive yourself for to live a life of peace?

_____

_____

_____

_____

_____

_____

_____

_____

_____

_____

_____

Good Morning…

Stop allowing yourself to believe you are not strong enough, smart enough, or brave enough to take on some of the hardest challenges in life. All the power has been with you since you were born. Tap into it any time.

What are your magical powers? How often do you really tap into them?

_____

_____

_____

_____

_____

_____

_____

_____

_____

_____

Good Morning...

When times get tough, do not give up, for the true blessing comes when you withstand the curves in life. You got this, no matter where you are on this journey. Never give up, for pacing yourself is what matters most.

How much do you believe in your prayers?

_____

_____

_____

_____

_____

_____

_____

_____

_____

_____

_____

Good Morning...

A determined person will always succeed, regardless of what is put along their path because they know the real meaning of pivoting. Be that person.

What is a big pivot you should be making to live a life of freedom?

_____

_____

_____

_____

_____

_____

_____

_____

_____

_____

_____

Good Morning...

Cherish the people you love most, for life is all about spreading love and inspiring others. Stop allowing materialistic items to dictate your happiness, for love defeats all.

What materialistic items do you have most connection to and why?

_____

_____

_____

_____

_____

_____

_____

_____

_____

_____

_____

_____

Good Morning...

Life should consist of smiles and laughter, as waking up daily is a blessing in itself. Do not allow the thieves of this society steal your positivity. Negativity will be temporary as long as you don't feed into it.

What has robbed you of your smile? How can you smile more in life?

_____

_____

_____

_____

_____

_____

_____

_____

_____

_____

_____

Good Morning…

If you continue to live by other people's rules or views, you will never succeed in life. Success means rising up without allowing the opinions of others to bring you down. With a clear mind and sincere heart, anything is possible.

What rules are you living by in life?

_____

_____

_____

_____

_____

_____

_____

_____

_____

_____

_____

_____

Good Morning...

Love wholeheartedly without any worries, for love is meant to be given unconditionally. I know past experiences may be preventing you from receiving or giving such an amazing gift. You are worth every second of love.

How does being loved unconditionally make you feel?

_____

_____

_____

_____

_____

_____

_____

_____

_____

_____

_____

Good Morning...

As the day progresses, take a few minutes to evaluate if are you truly living for yourself or you are living for others.

Are you living for yourself or others? What changes can you make to live for yourself?

_____

_____

_____

_____

_____

_____

_____

_____

_____

_____

_____

Good Morning...

This life will consume you in the worst way if you allow it. Allow your heart to be open to love knowing that is the only way to live, for love saves us all.

What has this life been telling you recently? Have you been listening?

_____

_____

_____

_____

_____

_____

_____

_____

_____

_____

_____

Good Morning...

Life is a journey filled with priceless moments and experiences that should never be wasted. Allow yourself to truly begin living, for life is such a precious gift we take for granted daily.

Are you just wasting time or living a life of happiness? What does your life look like at this moment?

_____

_____

_____

_____

_____

_____

_____

_____

_____

_____

_____

_____

Good Morning...

Live like there is no tomorrow and always smile knowing you can inspire someone's day. We, as humans, forget the simplest things make the world go round. Stop allowing your life to be dictated by the unnecessary and feed your life with what it needs to truly grow: LOVE

How does love flow in your everyday living?

_____

_____

_____

_____

_____

_____

_____

_____

_____

_____

_____

Good Morning...

May you awake daily ready for the world. Protect your energy knowing you are a sacred being filled with life. Pay attention and never allow your intuition to stir you wrong. You know what is right for you.

What are you doing to protect your energy today?

_____

_____

_____

_____

_____

_____

_____

_____

_____

_____

_____

Good Morning…

While you are in the darkness, it is hard to see, but know the light is right inside of you. The peace and stillness is thriving inside of you. Embrace yourself for the person you are.

What do you do in moments of stillness or is your mind still going? What thoughts consume your mind on a regular basis?

_____

_____

_____

_____

_____

_____

_____

_____

_____

_____

Good Morning...

Accepting differences is one of the main components of life that we often take for granted. Learn to open your mind and heart in ways you never imagined, for the world is one beautiful place if you can accept change.

What makes it so hard to accept differences?

_____

_____

_____

_____

_____

_____

_____

_____

_____

_____

_____

_____

Good Morning...

Learn to be more mindful with your words and actions. They can have an effect on someone else's life in major ways. The decision of it being a positive or negative impact is solely up to you.

How has mindfulness been incorporated in your life?

_____

_____

_____

_____

_____

_____

_____

_____

_____

_____

_____

Good Morning...

It is time to live daily to your own expectations; not letting society dictate the person you need to become. Break out the norm and be proud of who you are, for you are in this world for a reason.

What does your norm consist of? Does it add growth to your life?

_____

_____

_____

_____

_____

_____

_____

_____

_____

_____

_____

Good Morning...

Be so involved in your evolution that you do not have time to entertain the nonsense. Be so caught up in loving yourself that you do not even hear it.

What is the nonsense you must stop listening to?

_____

_____

_____

_____

_____

_____

_____

_____

_____

_____

_____

Good Morning…

This is your life and how you live it is your choice. No more blaming others for your unhappiness or finding reasons to live in your darkness. Use those reasons to fuel your guide to the light.

What better choices will you be making for your life starting today?

_____

_____

_____

_____

_____

_____

_____

_____

_____

_____

_____

Good Morning...

You are an exceptional asset to this world accomplishing all things you desire without fear. It is so admirable to watch you unfold as you have entered your best year yet.

What would your best year look like to you?

_____

_____

_____

_____

_____

_____

_____

_____

_____

_____

_____

Good Morning...

We allow fears and traumas to dictate our lives causing the shackles to be placed on us without allowing us to move in the direction we deeply desire. You are only stunting your growth, for love is your way out.

What do you choose for your life today?

_____

_____

_____

_____

_____

_____

_____

_____

_____

_____

_____

_____

Good Morning...

Misery loves company, so I challenge you daily to find a reason to smile and hold on to it, for positivity will always outweigh any kind of negativity.

Why is it hard for you to smile at times?

_____

_____

_____

_____

_____

_____

_____

_____

_____

_____

_____

Good Morning...

Live each day compassionately, for misery is a toxic drug that many choose to live by. It is time to overcome everything and smile, for life shouldn't be wasted.

How can misery be considered as a toxic drug in your life?

_____

_____

_____

_____

_____

_____

_____

_____

_____

_____

_____

Good Morning...

Today is such a beautiful day given with reasons. Take advantage of all the positivity and continue spreading the gift of love, for it truly conquers all.

How does love conquer all?

_____

_____

_____

_____

_____

_____

_____

_____

_____

_____

_____

_____

Good Morning...

As the days continue to pass you by, love is what truly keeps your heart smiling. We place so much thought onto temporary things or people without spreading the main source of life: LOVE. Fill your heart with joy, laughter, and happiness, for love can outweigh the test of times.

What provides you with the main source of living? How does this source provide you with more life?

_____

_____

_____

_____

_____

_____

_____

_____

_____

_____

_____

Good Morning...

Always remember this day was given with reason. Complications and battles are consistent reminders that you are still living. No one said it would be easy, but in the midst of your difficult times take a moment to smile, for optimism is an essential key to life.

What is an essential key in your life?

_____

_____

_____

_____

_____

_____

_____

_____

_____

_____

Good Morning...

May your day be filled with laughter and fun, for life's greatest moments are not captured with a camera but captured within our hearts.

What are the greatest moments captured in your heart?

_____

_____

_____

_____

_____

_____

_____

_____

_____

_____

_____

Good Morning...

Never allow a moment in life to be wasted, for each moment lost you cannot regain back.

Name a moment you wish you could relive again and why.

Good Morning…

Take each day straight on, for this day was provided due to the strength and endurance you have stored. Always have faith in your abilities and never forget everything happens for a reason.

Why are trials and obstacles so discouraging, while failure is a step towards success?

_____

_____

_____

_____

_____

_____

_____

_____

_____

_____

_____

Good Morning...

Take advantage of your talents and creativity, for you are better, stronger, and wiser than you have ever been. No time to doubt yourself now.

What is causing you to doubt yourself today?

_____

_____

_____

_____

_____

_____

_____

_____

_____

_____

_____

Good Morning...

Smiling is contagious, so don't be afraid to continue showing that flawless smile of yours, for it has the power to impact the lives of many.

How can your smile impact the lives around you?

_____

_____

_____

_____

_____

_____

_____

_____

_____

_____

_____

Good Morning...

Take a moment to cherish all you have been blessed with. Throughout life, we get caught up on materialistic things when true happiness is a result of what money can't buy.

Name all the things you cherish that money cannot buy.

_____

_____

_____

_____

_____

_____

_____

_____

_____

_____

_____

Good Morning...

Love freely without any restrictions, for regrets of steps we did not take will continue to linger in our hearts forever.

What steps are you taking towards creating more love in your life?

_____

_____

_____

_____

_____

_____

_____

_____

_____

_____

_____

_____

Good Morning...

As life continues to unfold, hold on to the things that truly make your heart come alive. For those moments are worth living for.

What are you living for?

_____

_____

_____

_____

_____

_____

_____

_____

_____

_____

_____

_____

Good Morning...

That moment you feel like your world is crumbling, stand strong,
for you were given this life with purpose. Doubt, worry, and stress
tend to fog your clarity, so stop what you're doing and focus on the
positive, for that will bring you brighter days ahead.

How do stress, worry, and doubt affect your life?

_____

_____

_____

_____

_____

_____

_____

_____

_____

_____

_____

_____

Good Morning…

Never be ashamed of the amazing person you truly are. Take a moment and look in the mirror, and see the beauty that radiates from inside of you. If no one else sees it, just know I do.

When you look in the mirror, what do you see? Try to see beyond your physical self to capture the real you.

_____

_____

_____

_____

_____

_____

_____

_____

_____

_____

_____

Good Morning...

Keep pushing and striving, for everything in life is earned not given. You will appreciate life so much more when you get to the finish line.

What finish line are you trying to cross?

_____

_____

_____

_____

_____

_____

_____

_____

_____

_____

_____

_____

Good Morning…

This world would not be complete without you. Your smile, your heart, and your personality are unmatched. You were meant for this life, so make sure to give it all you have.

What is your personality? Do you like who you are?

_____

_____

_____

_____

_____

_____

_____

_____

_____

_____

_____

_____

Good Morning...

Your knowledge, advice, and love allow the lives around you to be at ease. Your energy alone allows others to break from the binds that have been obstructing their growth. You are evolving and that alone, by love, is beauty within itself.

Describe the beauty that is inside of you.

_____

_____

_____

_____

_____

_____

_____

_____

_____

_____

_____

Good Morning…

There are no rights or wrongs in this world. Only lessons. Be easy on your spirit, for everyone makes mistakes.

What mistakes have you not forgiven yourself for?

_____

_____

_____

_____

_____

_____

_____

_____

_____

_____

_____

_____

Good Morning...

Increase your awareness while becoming the best you. Strip yourself of the layers that no longer serve you stepping into your rightful place in this world. You deserve it.

What layers of yourself are you working on stripping away?

_____

_____

_____

_____

_____

_____

_____

_____

_____

_____

_____

_____

Good Morning...

There will be times of brokenness, but those are the times that teach us the most valuable lessons. See the light in every dark corner knowing you are being set up for higher places.

Take this time to describe the dark and light side of you. Remember, it is called balance, so make sure to honor both parts.

_____

_____

_____

_____

_____

_____

_____

_____

_____

_____

Good Morning...

When life tries to throw you a curve ball, pick it up and throw it back. Refuse to allow anything to come into your world that you do not belong. You are bigger than any problem thrown at you. Start believing it.

What coping skills do you use when curve balls are thrown your way?

_____

_____

_____

_____

_____

_____

_____

_____

_____

_____

_____

Good Morning...

Our future is in front of us, not behind. The past is over now and what happened has been learned. Use this knowledge to break the everlasting cycle of trauma and shame.

What causes you to feel shameful in life?

_____

_____

_____

_____

_____

_____

_____

_____

_____

_____

_____

Good Morning...

Be proud of who you are without allowing society to commend you for being uniquely different. It is time we removed our whole mask to the world and expose our true selves.

What mask did you have to wear today?

_____

_____

_____

_____

_____

_____

_____

_____

_____

_____

_____

Good Morning...

You are right where you need to be. The unknown is your friend. You are entering the best chapter of your life as you read this. Are you ready?

If you knew the unknown could not break you, how would you approach it?

_____

_____

_____

_____

_____

_____

_____

_____

_____

_____

_____

_____

Good Morning...

As time continues to wait for no one, never lose sight of the motivation inside of you to want more. Failing is an example of trying, so never let them stir you wrong.

What is something you tried out and learned a mighty lesson from?

_____

_____

_____

_____

_____

_____

_____

_____

_____

_____

_____

_____

Good Morning…

Life is meant to be enjoyed. Just remember most of the problems in our lives are due to reactions to circumstances or situations. Think before reacting, for living with your ego can cause damage to your life.

How does your reaction to things dictate your life?

_____

_____

_____

_____

_____

_____

_____

_____

_____

_____

_____

_____

Good Morning...

Life is what you make it. We, as humans, need to understand life will not always be what we imagine it to be, but that should never stop us. For when you feel like you cannot give anymore is when your true blessing is near.

Why do you give up at times when things get tough?

_____

_____

_____

_____

_____

_____

_____

_____

_____

_____

_____

Good Morning...

Love with all you have. If you are passionate about something or someone, speak about it. If you need to express yourself on any level, do it. No point in holding on and having consistent weight on your shoulders. Release it, for life is what you make it.

What causes you to hold back so much? Are you fearful of love?

_____

_____

_____

_____

_____

_____

_____

_____

_____

_____

_____

_____

Good Morning...

No longer happy? You have the ability to change that. Tired of the inconsistency in your life? Move on and find something better. Don't feel like you can go on anymore? Well, think again. Stand back up and face it head-on, for the true power of growth and/or change comes from one's mindset.

What is it about life that keeps you away from fully being happy?

_____

_____

_____

_____

_____

_____

_____

_____

_____

_____

Good Morning…

Don't ever be afraid to express how you feel, for the weight of the world should not be consistently on your shoulders. We were given the ability to speak our minds for mighty reasons. The power to dictate how we feel lies inside us all.

How has your journey made you better?

_____

_____

_____

_____

_____

_____

_____

_____

_____

_____

_____

_____

Good Morning...

When the hardships begin to pour in, and you feel like your world is coming to end... Don't panic, for pain is meant to be felt. Not letting yourself sulk in the pain makes the difference. Transform that energy to regain your power. Life is all about perspective.

How do you transform your energy when feeling pain?

_____

_____

_____

_____

_____

_____

_____

_____

_____

_____

_____

Good Morning...

As life takes its course, make sure to remain in tune to what your body needs. Neglecting it causes sickness and unwanted emotions. You always deserve to be your best self.

How often do you listen to your body? Are you giving it what it needs?

_____

_____

_____

_____

_____

_____

_____

_____

_____

_____

_____

_____

Good Morning...

The world is very diversified with endless opportunities. It is time to let your mind expand without any bonds or chains. You are only as good as you give yourself credit for.

How much credit do you give yourself on a daily basis?

_____

_____

_____

_____

_____

_____

_____

_____

_____

_____

_____

Good Morning...

Life is one big gift waiting to be unfolded. Make sure to unravel it the way you desire.

What gift are you waiting for to be unfolded?

_____

_____

_____

_____

_____

_____

_____

_____

_____

_____

_____

_____

Good Morning…

You must overcome your dark days to get to your light. You must experience difficulties to appreciate life. You must let go to find yourself. Reminding your soul daily that you are enough.

What difficulties did you have to experience to find your light?

_____

_____

_____

_____

_____

_____

_____

_____

_____

_____

_____

_____

Good Morning...

In moments of uncertainty, we tend to doubt and worry causing us to go down the wrong path more frequently. If we continue to believe, have hope, and keep trying, the outcome will be so much worthwhile. Hold on, for better days are coming.

What same road have you been going down? When will you learn to break the cycle?

_____

_____

_____

_____

_____

_____

_____

_____

_____

_____

Good Morning...

Each day provided has its mixture of highs and lows. The way you manage them determines how they turn out to be.

How well do you manage everyday life?

_____

_____

_____

_____

_____

_____

_____

_____

_____

_____

_____

_____

Good Morning...

Life is one rocky journey filled with priceless memories one should always cherish and hold on to. So, today, I challenge you to laugh more and see the positivity in every situation. For there are reasons for your circumstances.

What keeps you laughing more?

_____

_____

_____

_____

_____

_____

_____

_____

_____

_____

_____

Good Morning...

Self-love is the best love and you can never give yourself too much of it. You are the most important on this planet. Treat yourself with the love and kindness you deserve to watch yourself blossom. It is such a beautiful process.

 What do you do to practice self-love during your hardest times?

_____

_____

_____

_____

_____

_____

_____

_____

_____

_____

_____

_____

Good Morning...

As materialistic and superficial items begin to be destroyed and many of our loved ones have been taken home, let us hold on to the priceless experiences and memories. The closest things or people in your life can never be replaced

What is a priceless experience you will remember for the rest of your life? How did it make you feel and who was involved?

_____

_____

_____

_____

_____

_____

_____

_____

_____

_____

_____

Good Morning...

As life continues to take its course, never be afraid to walk that extra mile, for your life can be transformed dramatically when fear does not exist.

If fear was a person, what would you say to it?

_____

_____

_____

_____

_____

_____

_____

_____

_____

_____

_____

Good Morning...

Be yourself in everything you do, for everything you do is a reflection of you.

What kind of reflection are you?

_____

_____

_____

_____

_____

_____

_____

_____

_____

_____

_____

_____

_____

Good Morning...

As time takes its toll on life, never let it change the wonderful person you are. You were created with lots of love and purpose. Don't ever lose sight of that, for your life is much more valuable than you can ever imagine.

Name a time where you lost sight of your purpose, but somehow still made it out on top.

_____

_____

_____

_____

_____

_____

_____

_____

_____

_____

Good Morning...

There are billions of people on this planet, but no one is as amazing as you. You are the definition of love. Your energy alone saves live. You bring the best out of people, and for that you should be honored.

Do you honor yourself? Why or why not?

_____

_____

_____

_____

_____

_____

_____

_____

_____

_____

_____

_____

Good Morning...

We cannot control the thoughts, feelings, or opinions of others, but we do have control over the way we react, respond, and acknowledge these individuals or situations. Live life with a clear mind and open heart, for you cannot establish growth by letting someone or something have power over you

Who do you allow to have power over you? Who has a negative effect on you?

_____

_____

_____

_____

_____

_____

_____

_____

_____

_____

Good Morning...

Some people criticize themselves causing way more damage than expected. It is time to lift yourself up today. Replace that negative mind with love to find the true meaning of contentment.

Do you enjoy just being content with life? Why or why not?

_____

_____

_____

_____

_____

_____

_____

_____

_____

_____

_____

Good Morning...

Forgive and let go, for continuing to hold on to grudges only stops your growth.

What about forgiveness do you still have trouble with?

_____

_____

_____

_____

_____

_____

_____

_____

_____

_____

_____

_____

Good Morning...

As your day begins, make sure to breathe in all the positivity in your life while releasing the negativity. Be thankful for this day given and live to your full potential, for living for others will never make you sincerely happy.

What's keeping you from doing things differently in life to create a better future?

_____

_____

_____

_____

_____

_____

_____

_____

_____

_____

_____

Good Morning...

As time continues and the world stops for no one, just remember you have everything needed to conquer right inside of you. Search deep to find it.

Do you believe you are equipped to conquer the world? Why or why not?

_____

_____

_____

_____

_____

_____

_____

_____

_____

_____

_____

Good Morning...

In society today, LOVE is misconstrued, while misery continues to have company. Stop defining people from their outward appearances while calling it love.

How does someone's outer appearance determine one's heart?

_____

_____

_____

_____

_____

_____

_____

_____

_____

_____

_____

_____

Good Morning...

Never give up on hope, for it's when times get extremely rough that you are being set up for something even greater.

What hope do you have for a better future?

_____

_____

_____

_____

_____

_____

_____

_____

_____

_____

_____

_____

Good Morning...

Never give up on hope, for it's when times get extremely rough that you are being set up for something even greater.

What hope do you have for a better future?

_____

_____

_____

_____

_____

_____

_____

_____

_____

_____

_____

_____

_____

You made it!!!!! You've finally decided to take your mask off to be real with the one person who matters most: YOURSELF!!! I cannot even put into words how proud I am of you for taking the time to connect to who you truly are.

Now, I want to ask you a few questions challenging you for yet another year of self-love and growth that you can take some alone time to complete:

How proud of yourself are you for completing this 365-day journey?

_____

_____

_____

_____

_____

How will you continue to incorporate self-love in your daily life?

_____

_____

_____

_____

_____

Where do you see yourself a year from now?

_____

_____

_____

_____

_____

_____

_____

_____

_____

_____

_____

_____

I hope this 365-day journey has brought you closer to yourself as the judgement and criticism fades to enter a world of complete love and light. Finding yourself is the best reward you can give to yourself and thank you for allowing *The Good Morning Text* to be your guide to getting there.

Why *The Good Morning Text* Was Written:

I wanted to share with you all the reason *The Good Morning Text* was even written. In 2013, my best friend was killed in an automotive accident that cost him his life. I will never forget that day. It was as if my heart was stolen right out my chest. I relived his tragedy time and time again not understanding how someone at the age of 25 can be taken so soon from us. I could not process the fact that he was no longer here causing two years of my life to be filled with complete darkness. I lost the very part of me that kept me going faking life continuously with a smile.

You see, Charlie was the definition of pure love. No matter how many times I messed up, he saw me for my true self and that alone I will cherish forever. It was not until two years after his death on the beach in Puerto Rico that I had this epiphany. It was as if God directly spoke to me and said "heal through writing." As you can see, writing had been a part of my life for years before, but not much effort was put into directing my emotions through this outlet.

After that one beautiful morning on the beach in Rincon, Puerto Rico, my life changed forever. I began healing myself with the words I continued to speak daily allowing my soul to release more and more of the tragedy as time went on. I would be lying if I said I did not miss him until this day, but one thing I do know is Charlie is with me every day guiding my way. I feel his presence with me daily and I am so lucky to have him as a part of me, even in the afterlife. The friendship we have is forever and has allowed me to blossom in such beautiful ways. It has allowed me to believe in my full potential and has set me free from the bondage of darkness I once lived in.

Charlie passed away July 15, 2013, and with this healing journey I knew it was only right to release the book on the day he died; changing my narrative to life. I choose to be free in love.

Thank you all for taking this journey with me. Be on the lookout for more LOVE to come.

More Information About the Author:

I am the creator of The Adored Project as well as the founder of Awakened Hearts Unite.

The Adored Project- @adoredbydanni

The Adored Project began two years after writing *The Good Morning Text* during a time in my life that I felt the darkness trying to take over. You see, it was the hurricane Maria that hit Puerto Rico in 2017 that tried to shake my life. My only living grandparent was living in Puerto Rico during that time.

When you have experienced depression growing up you know the feeling all too well. That is how The Adored Project was created in September 2017 during yet again a moment of darkness in my life. It was created to shed light and love upon my own life in hopes my love would spread in the process. I felt myself falling in the dark hole, not knowing where to go, turning to love as my answer. I provided love to receive love to not be subjected to the darkness any longer.

You see, the power of love is real and can change lives forever. Each heart is written to myself in hopes that my words can impact someone else. Each heart given allows the power of love to be shared to make this world a better place.

A month after the hurricane hit was when we finally heard back from my Wela and The Adored Project has been thriving ever since reaching over 10,000 hearts given all over the world. I honestly believe in my heart that with love this world will be a better place for you and I. Be on the lookout for more love to come, as the only limitation in life is myself.

Awakened Hearts Unite

Awakened Hearts Unite was created January 2020 during a time I felt more love was needed to be shared in the world, not knowing the chaos that was upon us. I knew the hearts I share in this world were designed for much more, as many of us during this time in our lives are awakening our hearts. We are awakening our hearts to heal and place more love into our own self. That was how I built AHU with the thought of unity of awakened hearts ready to heal, grow, and love together to make this world a better place.

Awakened Hearts Unite is a safe space where judgment and criticism does not exist. I do not claim to heal anyone during these sessions, but I am a firm believer that with more self-love we can all heal ourselves. With times like these, AHU has pivoted to the virtual world. Meet me virtually as we become our best selves flourishing and loving ourselves to make this world a better place.

For more information on both The Adored Project and Awakened Hearts Unite, please follow on social media @adoredbydanni.

Love is the Only Way Out!

Made in the USA
Middletown, DE
27 February 2021

34390231R00214